Dog Basics

The essential guide to caring for your dog

Caroline Davis

hamlyn

A Pyramid Paperback

First published in Great Britain in 2007 by
Hamlyn, a division of Octopus Publishing Group Ltd
2–4 Heron Quays, London E14 4JP

Copyright © Octopus Publishing Group Ltd 2007

This material was previously published as *Essential Dog*.

Distributed in the United States and Canada by
Sterling Publishing Co., Inc.
387 Park Avenue South, New York, NY 10016–8810

ISBN-13: 978-0-600-61463-0
ISBN-10: 0-600-61463-8

A CIP catalogue record for this book is available from the
British Library

Printed in China

10 9 8 7 6 5 4 3 2 1

The advice given here should not be used as a substitute for
that of a veterinary surgeon. No dogs or puppies were harmed
in the making of this book. In this book, unless the information provided is specifically for female dogs, dogs are referred
to throughout as 'he'. The information is equally applicable to
both male and female dogs, unless otherwise specified.

CONTENTS

INTRODUCTION

As I write, there is a dog curled up next to me, a German Shepherd Dog called Hal. Our family has had the pleasure of his company for some eight years or so now and, for us, Hal represents everything about a dog that owners could wish for. He is gentle and good-natured, playful and obedient, and has his own unique character that we have come to understand and appreciate over the years. As I look at him, all the reasons for owning a dog are clear: quite simply, he is a fantastic pal.

For many people, young and old alike, and particularly those who live alone, their dog is their best friend — and there are many reasons for this. A dog is the ultimate companion. He won't judge our sins, real or imagined, get angry with us, lie to us or cheat us. He may, of course, be miserable if we treat him badly, but he will never blame us — his innocence and trust is complete.

It is a well-known fact that dogs are great stress-relievers. Dogs are more willing and receptive to your emotions than humans: who else will happily listen to your moans and groans day in and day out, celebrate with you when no one else is there to share special moments, and comfort you in hours of need.

There are few things more relaxing than getting home from a hard day's work and being welcomed by a creature that is absolutely ecstatic to see you, then taking him for a walk to relieve your mental strains and physical aches.

However, in order to achieve a rewarding and a problem-free relationship with a dog, it is essential to realize that having some inkling of how a dog thinks and feels goes a long way to achieving success in these departments. As with anything in life, the more you put into something, the more you get out of it.

Successful relationships are based on positive two-way communication and respect. By being a fair and positive leader to your dog, you can define a code of practice and behaviour that your dog understands and responds to in the way that you would wish. You can shape your new friend into a well-mannered adult that you can be proud of and everyone will admire, love and want to own. Your dog deserves no less.

This book shows that there are many aspects to dog ownership, and there may be topics covered that you have never previously thought about. Prospective owners who read it will see that they must carefully consider all of those elements before taking the plunge and getting a dog, for their own and the animal's sake. While I hope that established owners may well find some information contained within this book invaluable in helping them achieve an even more rewarding and enjoyable relationship with their pet.

INITIAL STEPS

The question you must ask yourself is: 'I may want a dog, but would a dog want me as his owner?' The decision to have a dog should be a family one. It should not be made lightly and without a great deal of thought. The dog, when you get him, will become an integral part of the family and is likely to remain so for many years. It is important, therefore, that every member of the immediate family should want a dog and be prepared to accept the duties that responsible ownership entails.

Why a dog?

Dogs are traditionally seen as the number one pet. Although the majority are kept as a source of enormous pleasure as a household pet, many dogs still perform the jobs they were originally bred to do. These tasks include herding and guarding duties, as well as being employed as 'eyes and ears' for people with sight and hearing impediments. Dogs are also used to great effect in search-and-rescue situations. All in all, dogs are the most versatile pet humans could wish for.

Owning and caring for a dog provides comfort and interest to the lives of people of all ages.

Companionship

In return for food, shelter and affection, dogs offer unconditional love and loyalty to their owners. Owning a happy, healthy dog is one of the most rewarding pleasures in life, and it gives you opportunities to make new friends while walking your pet and taking him to training classes. Having a dog – as with other pets – also has an advantageous effect in helping people relax and recover from illness, as well as keeping us alert and lively as we age.

Exercise and enjoyment

Walking the dog is not only essential for his well-being, it is also excellent for our health. Just a couple of 20-minute brisk walks help to tone our bodies and maintain cardiovascular fitness. Playing with and training a dog is good fun for both parties. Few things are more entertaining than a session of playing 'fetch' with a ball.

Affection

A dog's love of affection from his owners is what makes him special to us; love and loyalty are high on the list of characteristics owners require in a dog. Naturally social creatures that evolved as pack animals, dogs just live to please their owners, because in return they are provided with everything they need to survive comfortably. Some types of dog are more affectionate than others, so people who require such a dog should read up on the various breeds to ensure they end up with a pet that adores being made a fuss of and petted, as opposed to one that prefers more restrained affection on its own terms.

Security and independence

There is no doubt that, for those who live on their own, having another living being in the home gives confidence. To ensure that your dog remains healthy means that you have to organize your life to a certain extent to accommodate him, and this in itself helps people to maintain direction and order in their lives.

Dogs are efficient warning systems too – they are quick to alert their owners to anything untoward such as a house fire, and have also been known to save people in other types of danger, such as the presence of intruders. It is their acute sense of

Dogs are good for your health: playing with and walking a dog ensures you get plenty of regular exercise.

hearing that has made dogs invaluable in their roles as hearing dogs for the deaf, while their trainability enables dogs to act as guides for visually impaired people as well as act as 'home helps' for the disabled.

Cross-breed or pedigree?

Before getting a dog, you will need to make a number of decisions, including selecting the breed and type of dog you would like. You may have in mind the ideal appearance, colour, type and temperament, but would the type of dog you have in mind fit without any problems into your family's lifestyle and fulfil your expectations?

What's the difference?

Picking a pedigree or non-pedigree dog is your decision. However, armed with a fair amount of knowledge you are in the best position to make an informed choice and, therefore, end up with a pet that fulfils all your basic requirements.

Some pedigree dogs are known for certain character traits, such as a laid-back attitude, tolerance and a strong affection for humans, and this can make the job of choosing a dog easier if you do your homework well.

The options

Dogs are available in three varieties:
• pure-bred (pedigree).
• cross-bred (pedigree parents of different breeds).
• mongrel (a dog with one or both parents cross-breds or mongrels).
Cost may influence your choice, but bear in mind that pure-breds are not necessarily superior to cross-breds or mongrels – indeed in terms of health the reverse is generally true, as many pure-bred dogs are prone to physical and psychological problems caused by inbreeding.

What's in a name?

Pedigree dog breeds are categorized into named groups to differentiate their particular uses, that is, what they were originally bred to do.

Longhaired breeds need correct grooming on a daily basis to remain matt-free, healthy and looking good.

Your lifestyle

This determines, to a great extent, what sort of pet you should be looking for. In the dog's lifetime, you are responsible for his health and well-being.
• Some breeds, compared with others, are high-maintenance, so only consider these types of dogs if you are able to provide daily care and attention for them for the next 15 years or so. If you get a dog with a coat that needs a lot of grooming, or requires clipping on a regular basis, you must be prepared to learn how to care for his coat properly.
• If you choose an extrovert, energetic type with high exercise needs, then you must have the time to cater for him. Such

PEDIGREE, CROSS-BREED OR NON-PEDIGREE?

TYPE	PROS	CONS
Pedigree  *Labrador Retriever*	• Having researched the breed, you usually know what to expect in terms of appearance and character. • There are many specific types and colours to choose from. • Pedigrees are usually raised with great care, so the animal should be healthy.	• Pedigrees are more expensive than cross-breeds. • Some breeds are prone to hereditary problems, or particular ailments. • Some breeds have particular character traits, or care needs, that may not be appealing, or practical for your lifestyle. • Certain breeds can be difficult to obtain as they are rare.
Cross-breed  *German Shepherd Cross*	• Usually less expensive than pedigrees. • Knowing the parents, you have a fair idea of the appearance and character. • Generally more hardy than pedigrees, but this does depend on the cross and the parentage. • Since crosses are usually intended, you can normally expect the puppies to have been raised with care and be well socialized and healthy; but this is not always the case, so beware.	• Not always easily available – especially if you want a particular cross-breed. • Certain combinations can be quite 'explosive', resulting in a highly demanding, exhausting or even daunting pet (for example a Border Collie x English Springer Spaniel – although there are always exceptions).
Non-pedigree  *Mongrel*	• Free, or inexpensive. • Wide type and colour choice. • Usually easily available. • Generally few health complications.	• The character traits of the parents are generally unknown, so, to an extent, how the dog will turn out in terms of looks, behaviour and character is uncertain. • You may have to wait a while to find the age, colour and sex of your choice. • You cannot always be sure that the animal has been properly raised and cared for, so look for signs of ill health, behaviour problems or character defects.

considerations may seem obvious, but animal welfare organizations still have to cope with thousands of unwanted animals that their owners felt unable to care for.

The right dog for you

Pedigree dogs are not necessarily more loving, clever or naughty than other dogs, and each breed's appearance is a matter of taste. Working dogs tend to be more demanding of their owners, companion dogs tend to be more laid-back and cross-breeds tend to be generally thought of as being 'hardy'. Whatever the type or breeding, an animal's character is also determined by the way it is reared and its handling by humans. Whether you get a pedigree or non-pedigree dog, the costs of neutering, vaccinating, feeding and caring for him will be just the same. The only difference will be in the initial cost of acquiring him.

The flow chart opposite is an at-a-glance guide to finding the right sort of dog to suit different lifestyles – theirs and yours – for a fulfilling and happy relationship.

BASIC GROUP CHARACTERISTICS

GROUP	CHARACTERISTICS
Pastoral dogs (German Shepherd, Collies, Sheepdogs, Newfoundland, Welsh Corgis, Briard.)	Responsive to training; very active by nature; extremely sensitive and prone to stereotypic behaviour if their intelligence and energy is not correctly handled; very loyal; need lots of exercise and mental stimulation.
Hounds (Greyhound, Beagle, Basenji, Dachshund, Rhodesian Ridgeback.)	Affectionate and friendly but highly independent, and therefore more difficult to train than dogs of other groups.
Gundogs (Pointers, Retrievers, Spaniels.)	Popular as companions, as their inbred instinct is to work on an individual basis with their owners; tend to be good-natured, tolerant, keen to please and quick to learn.
Terriers (Bedlington Terrier, Bull Terrier, Australian Terrier, German Hunting Terrier, Jack Russell Terrier.)	Lively, curious and tenacious with strong and determined personalities; often 'bossy', quite vocal; may be suspicious of strangers and not always tolerant of children.
Working dogs (Rottweiler, Dobermann, Leonberger, Boxer, Siberian Husky, St Bernard, Pyrenean Mountain Dog, Japanese Akita, Dogue de Bordeaux, Great Dane.)	Temperament will be influenced by their breeding, environment/socialization and upbringing; tend to be strong-willed and can be become 'too big for their boots' if not handled appropriately.
Toy dogs (Pekingese, Pomeranian, Miniature Pinscher, Cavalier King Charles Spaniel, Yorkshire Terrier.)	Small in size and generally friendly and affectionate, though can be brave watchdogs.

Airedale Terrier

WHAT TYPE OF DOG WILL SUIT YOUR LIFESTYLE?

Young active couple; large house; remote rural area; lots of off-lead exercise opportunity.	➤	Experienced owners; require watchdog/ security and companionship.	➤

Hair and slobber OK ➤ Briard, Rough Collie, German Shepherd Dog, Newfoundland, St Bernard, Leonberger, Afghan Hound, Borzoi, Scottish Deerhound.

▲

Medium to giant dog preferred

▼

Prefer easy-care coat ➤ Rhodesian Ridgeback, Great Dane, Rottweiler, Lurcher, Bloodhound, Shorthaired German Shepherd Dog, English Springer Spaniel, Irish Wolfhound, Setters and Pointers, Dobermann, Bullmastiff.

Active person; small house and garden; built-up residential area; off-lead exercise necessitates care. ➤ Experienced owner; requires active, happy pet for companionship and exercise. ➤

Requires easy-care smooth coat ➤ Whippet, Lancashire Heeler, Jack Russell Terrier, Chihuahua, Shorthaired Dachshund, Boston Terrier.

▲

Small dog preferred

▼

No objection to grooming ➤ Miniature/Toy Poodle, Cavalier/King Charles Spaniel, Pomeranian, Yorkshire Terrier, Maltese, Affenpinscher, West Highland White Terrier, American/English Cocker Spaniel, Dandie Dinmont Terrier, Border Terrier, Bedlington Terrier.

Middle-aged couple; average-sized house and large garden in rural area; enjoy walking and home travel. ➤ Experienced owners; require kind, fun, active dog for outings and companionship. ➤

Medium maintenance coat OK ➤ Rough Collie, English Cocker/Springer Spaniel, Standard Poodle, Border Collie, Golden Retriever, Airedale Terrier, Schnauzers, Siberian Husky, Setters.

▲

Medium to large dog preferred

▼

Prefer easy-care coat ➤ Dalmatian, Labrador Retriever, Weimeraner, Rottweiler, Smooth Collie, Basenji, Dobermann, Boxer, Greyhound, Shorthaired German Shepherd Dog, Pointers, Hungarian Vizsla, Pharoah Hound, Rhodesian Ridgeback.

Family with young children; large house and garden; residential area. ➤ First-time owners; require friendly and fun family companion and watchdog. ➤

Medium maintenance coat OK ➤ Bearded Collie, Newfoundland, Shetland Sheepdog, Rough Collie, Cavalier/King Charles Spaniel, Tibetan Spaniel, Bernese Mountain Dog, Golden Retriever, Swedish Vallhund.

▲

Medium to large dog preferred

▼

Prefer easy-care coat ➤ Dalmatian, Labrador Retriever, Boxer, Smooth Collie, Greyhound, Schipperke, Boston Terrier, Whippet, Beagle.

Senior couple; limited mobility; small house and garden. ➤ Owned dogs on and off throughout life; require loyal, affectionate pet and watchdog. ➤

High coat maintenance OK ➤ Lhasa Apso, Shih Tzu, Bichon Frise, Miniature/Toy Poodle, Cavalier/King Charles Spaniel, Maltese, Longhaired Dachshund, Pekingese, Papillon.

▲

Any size OK but small preferred

▼

Prefer easy-care coat ➤ Greyhound, Schipperke, Corgi, Pug, Chihuahua, Italian Greyhound, Chinese Crested, Dandie Dinmont Terrier.

Puppy or adult?

Many people only think of getting a puppy, but that may not be the best choice for their circumstances or lifestyle; the character of an older dog is easier to see and any difficult or undesirable traits will already be apparent.

PUPPY OR ADULT: AT-A-GLANCE GUIDE

AGE	PROS	CONS
Puppy	• Puppies and young adults tend to be more adaptable than their mature counterparts, but it really does depend on many circumstances and characters. • You can enjoy seeing a puppy grow and develop. • You will, hopefully, have many years to enjoy together. • To a great extent, it will be easier to train him to behave in the way you require.	• A young puppy needs small feeds at regular intervals during the day at first, opportunities to go outside to relieve himself after meals and plenty of attention in order to shape desirable behaviour and properly socialize him, all of which are time-consuming. • A puppy may find it frightening to be introduced into a busy family unless he has been brought up in such an environment and been well socialized with humans (and possibly other pets) since birth. • If there are young children in the house, they will need a good deal of supervision while around and handling the puppy to ensure he is not inadvertently hurt or tormented. • He will not have been neutered.
Adult	• Not as time-consuming as a puppy. • He is likely to have been house-trained. • Character established. • Potentially socialized with people and other animals. • He may have been obedience-trained. • Potentially neutered.	• Limited lifespan depending on age. • He may take longer to bond with you and other pets. • An adult may be more difficult to integrate into your family. • He may have some illness or some established condition. • He may have undesirable behaviour traits that only become apparent when he has settled into your home.

If you already have a dog, ensure that a new pet does not prefer to spend more time with your dog than with you.

Dogs and children

Young children cannot be expected to know how to approach and handle a dog correctly, so it is imperative that they are supervised at all times when together to prevent accidents. Naturally, children want to explore their new pet and play with him, but poking him in the ear or disturbing him when he is eating or sleeping are certainly not the best way to do this.

If your children are taught how to handle dogs with gentleness and respect, then most children and dogs become the best of friends. See pages 60–61 for more detailed information on this subject.

Which sex?

If your dog or puppy is to be neutered, then the question of its sex becomes less important as there will be little difference between males and females. How loving and obedient the dog will be depends on how he is brought up and treated by his owner. See pages 110–111 for detailed information on neutering.

One dog or two?

Is it a good idea to get another dog as a companion for your existing one? Having two dogs can usually work very well for all concerned once they have accepted each other. It can also have drawbacks if you do not take care to make sure that they do not bond closer to each other than to you. You may end up with problems in training them, and in their learning undesirable traits from each other. See pages 54–55 for more detailed information on this subject.

When to get a dog

You may want a dog, but think – would a dog want to be with you right at this moment in your life? Wanting a dog and getting one are two very different things. Whether you choose an adult dog or a puppy, you must take into account your personal circumstances at the relevant time. There are many things to consider before welcoming a dog into your home.

Get the timing right

Are you ready to get a dog? The time may not be ideal to get one if you are:
• moving house or due to go on holiday.
• busy at work and socially.
• changing jobs or facing job loss.
• in the throes of an illness.
• separating from your partner or suffering bereavement.
• expecting a new baby.
• approaching a big family celebration that will disturb your routines and increase household activity or noise levels.

There are always exceptions, and many people find comfort in their pets at times when they are suffering stress. Such owners may feel that, although they are in turmoil, their pets are not suffering because they remain fed and cared for. However, pets do feel their owners' anxieties and can worry. These anxieties may manifest in behaviour such as attention-seeking or soiling around the home.

It is important that you are in a position both materially and emotionally to offer a secure and harmonious home to a new dog.

Holidays

Wait until you have been away before getting a dog, because otherwise he will suffer upheaval twice in a very short space of time – initially when you remove him from his former home, and then when you disappear and leave him in a boarding kennels or with a carer. To remain mentally and physically well, a new pet needs a good deal of time to settle in and feel secure in his new home.

Dog availability

It is sometimes not as easy to get a dog as you may imagine for several reasons:
• If you want a particular breed, colour or sex of dog, it may not be available and you may have to register a specific requirement with a breeder so that when an animal is available you have first choice.
• Puppy availability always depends on breeding seasons.
• There may not immediately be the exact type of dog you want at rescue centres.
• Puppies tend to be in high demand at rescue centres and you may have to wait.

Ensure it is the right time to get a dog for all the family.

Where to get a dog

There are many avenues to investigate when searching for a dog – from pedigree breeders and owners of a mongrel that has produced puppies to a rescue centre. It helps to be fully informed of all possible advantages and disadvantages before you decide.

Finding a dog

Your local paper, pet stores, vet surgery notice boards, dog magazines, word of mouth and rescue centres are all potential ways of finding an adult dog or puppy.

Which source is best?

There are several considerations to take into account with all of them, as described below, and no one source is best.

Dog breeders

When choosing a puppy, try to select him from a whole litter. The appearance of the young puppies will influence your choice, but so too should their behaviour and health; it is preferable to pick one that is healthy, outgoing, frisky and friendly. Don't pick an animal that looks unhealthy.

Sometimes it is possible to get an older pedigree dog from a breeder who has no further use for it, or puppies resulting from accidental matings that are therefore not suitable for breeding.

Friends and family

An older, house- and obedience-trained dog can be a good idea if you do not have the time to spend training a puppy.

Rescue centres or animal welfare shelters

If you opt for an animal shelter or rescue centre, find out as much as you can about the dog from the staff. A former stray dog, for example, may not be house-trained.

Strays

You may come across a dog that you think has been abandoned, however someone could be grieving for their lost pet. Try to trace his owners through local authorities and animal welfare shelters; put up 'found' posters in local veterinary surgeries and shops and have him checked for a microchip.

Pet stores or 'puppy farms'

Buying a dog from a pet store or 'puppy farm' is not recommended. If this is your only option, ensure that the animals are cared for, have adequate space, food and water and appear healthy.

HOW MUCH WILL A DOG COST?

SOURCE	COST
Pedigree breeder	Depending on the breed and whether or not the dog is of show quality, prices range enormously.
Friends and family	Non-pedigree puppies or adults are generally free 'to good homes'; part-pedigree and pedigrees can vary in cost depending on the reason for re-homing.
Rescue centre	There is generally a charge to cover the cost of neutering and vaccinations.
Strays	Free.
Pet store	Prices vary: pedigree dogs are more expensive.

Essential equipment

There is a huge, bewildering range of equipment and products designed specially for dogs – many described as something your pet just can't live without. Many of these items are simply not essential, however. You won't need a great deal of equipment to care for your new adult dog or puppy, and what you actually do need tends not to be very expensive.

Food and water bowls should be large enough for your size of dog to eat and drink from.

Food and water bowls

Your dog should have his own food and water bowls that cannot be tipped over. Glazed ceramic or stainless steel bowls are the best as they can be cleaned most hygienically and cannot be chewed, but plastic will do.

Poop scoops

Poop scoops are designed to pick up your dog's faeces hygienically so that you can dispose of the waste, both in the garden and out on walks. Dispose of faeces, wrapped up in newspaper or biodegradable bags, with the rubbish, not down the toilet. When out on walks, carry a biodegradable plastic bag to put the faeces in and take it home to dispose of, or place it in a dog waste bin.

Bed and bedding

Choose a bed that will be big enough for the dog when he is fully grown, with raised sides to protect against draughts, and made of easily washed material (see chart opposite). Bedding should be thick enough for him to lie on comfortably, and of an easy-wash, quick-dry material. Blankets, fleece, old duvets, an old pillow and fleecy veterinary pet bedding all make good, insulating bedding for dogs.

Toys

Throwing toys will entice most dogs to play, as it alerts their chase-catch instinct, and you can use this instinct to help train your dog to retrieve and recall. Hiding toys for them to sniff

Buy a bed that will be large enough for the dog to lie down in comfortably when he is mature.

BEDS AND BEDDING: AT-A-GLANCE GUIDE

BED TYPE	PROS	CONS
Cardboard box	• Cheap • Readily available • High sides keep out draughts.	• Needs replacing regularly • Needs extra bedding • Easily chewed.
Plastic	• Inexpensive • Hygienic • Easy to clean • High-sided types keep out draughts.	• Needs extra bedding • Easily chewed.
Wicker	• Looks attractive.	• Expensive • Draughty • Harbours dust and fur; difficult to clean • Needs extra bedding • Easily chewed.
Cushioned or fake-fur bed	• Comfortable • No extra bedding usually needed.	• Can harbour fleas if not washed regularly • Can be difficult to wash and dry • Expensive • Easily chewed.
Bean bags	• Dogs love them • Comfortable • Warm.	• Removing the polystyrene beads in order to wash the cover takes time • If the beads escape they can take hours to clear up • Easily chewed.

out and grab satisfies their scent trail-stalk and catch-kill instincts. Shaking a toy is their way of stunning the 'prey' or causing fatal injuries, making it less likely to fight back. Chewing a toy, or ripping it to shreds satisfies their instincts to rip off chunks of flesh.

There is a huge variety of toys specially designed for dogs, ranging for balls on ropes for throwing and fetching to hiding toys for them to sniff out.

Activity toys and chews will keep your dog occupied. Activity toys are designed to have biscuits put inside them, keeping your dog busy for ages. Chews must be suitably sized for the dog, and must only be given under supervision, to avoid choking.

Canine first-aid kit

This is essential both for treating minor injuries and when you may need to administer emergency first-aid until a vet takes over. You can purchase ready-assembled first-aid kits from pet stores, or from your vet. See page 117 for detailed information on the basic contents required when putting together a first-aid kit.

Parasite treatments

Parasites, both internal and external, have a detrimental effect on your dog's health. The most efficient treatments are available on prescription from vets, and it is worth spending a little bit more on these as they work eminently better than many shop-bought products. See page 104.

Collars

The most suitable collars are the broad leather or fabric ones or the half-check (check-choke), which is three-quarters nylon or leather and a quarter chain link. Half-checks are good when training, because you can achieve a rattle with the chain part to attract the dog's attention.

When fitting a collar, make sure you can slide two fingers between it and the dog's neck. Check the collar regularly for signs of chafing, and also to see that it still fits comfortably on a growing dog.

Leash

Leashes, like collars, are available in all sorts of lengths and designs. What is important, however, is to choose the most appropriate one for you and your dog. It makes an enormous difference for both parties in terms of comfort and control if you have a leash that is the correct length for the size of your dog, and the right width for your hand.

The leash must be of suitable length to maintain a slack tension. If it is too short,

WARNING

Choke chains are not advisable, as they are too easy to use inappropriately and cause discomfort or even damage to your dog.

the dog will be dragged along; too long and you will have metres of lead to deal with. Choose a fabric or leather lead that can be extended or shortened as desired (as favoured by dog trainers), and then you will have the best of both worlds when training and when simply out for a walk.

Retractable leashes are available in a variety of designs, but as some are better than others it is imperative that you choose one you can retract easily and instantly when desired. You must also buy the variety suited to the weight of your dog, otherwise it may not be strong enough to control him (some have been reported to snap when under stress and flick back into the handler's body or face, resulting in serious injury). To be on the safe side, do not use retractable leads on dogs that pull or become very excitable.

Crate

Also called a den or a cage, a crate serves as a bed and is useful for toilet training, for keeping the dog separate from the family and other pets when necessary, and for safety when travelling with your dog. Crates

There's a wide choice of collars and leashes available. For ease and effectiveness of handling and training make sure you choose the right ones. Head collars like the 'Halti' and 'Gentle Leader' are great options.

A wide-toothed comb (left) helps de-mat tangles in long coats; a slicker brush (centre) is good at removing dead hair; and a flea comb (right) will help remove fleas from the coat.

come in all sizes, with different types of opening. Good, sturdy ones are expensive, so choose one that will be big enough to accommodate your dog when it is fully grown. Cheap crates tend to be badly made or flimsy, and therefore represent poor economy because they do not last.

Plastic-covered metal crates are quieter and easier to clean than those constructed out of bare or galvanized metal. A two-door foldaway crate is more convenient, especially when being used in a vehicle.

Grooming gear

All dogs should be groomed regularly, but some breeds need to be groomed more often than others, in order to keep the coat and skin in good condition, to maintain appearance, to minimize shedding of hair around the home and to prevent matting.

For short-coated breeds, a stiff brush is best. For a medium-length coat, a stiff brush and a hound glove (a silky glove used to give a gloss to the coat) are ideal. To deal with tangles in a long coat, a metal, wide-toothed comb is essential. Your dog's breeder and/or local canine beauty salon will advise on the best tools for your dog's coat.

Owners of breeds that require regular clipping, stripping or trimming sometimes need to invest in the tools required to do this at home rather than visiting a professional dog groomer every few weeks. This can be economical if you want to keep your pet's coat at a manageable and suitable length rather than having it professionally styled. However, 'professional grooming' is harder than it looks; there is a knack to it, so you will have to be shown how to do it in order to get a decent-looking result.

Kennel and run

A kennel or run can be a useful option for several reasons:
• If your dog is a habitual escape artist when in the garden.
• To allow the dog to dry off after a wet, muddy walk.
• To control your dog when you have visitors who are afraid of other dogs, or don't like them.
• To control your dog when visitors bring their own dog(s), and your dog doesn't get on with them.
• To let your dog have somewhere to rest in peace when necessary.

Feeding your dog

To maintain your dog's good health, it is essential to feed him both a well-balanced diet and the right amount of it on a daily basis. There is a wide range of canine foods available, so it can be difficult deciding which variety or make is the best choice for your dog. There are, however, certain dietary nutrients that a dog cannot do without, as well as age, health and lifestyle considerations to take into account, and this makes the job of deciding on the most suitable diet much easier.

Eating habits

Dogs are omnivorous and can be kept on specially formulated vegetarian diets, although they do prefer meat-based foods. In a wild state the dog hunts, kills, feeds, then rests. He may gorge himself on a whole animal one day, then go without food for the next two or three; this is why many dogs eat until they are fit to burst – instinct tells them they may have to wait quite a while before their next meal.

Adult dogs are usually fed once a day, but splitting that feed into two meals adds interest. It is also better to feed certain deep-chested breeds (such as German Shepherd Dogs, Great Danes and Setters) several small meals rather than one big one, to avoid serious digestive ailments such as bloat (gastric dilation and volvulus).

Commercially produced clinical diets are available (usually only from vets), which can help dogs suffering from such diseases as kidney stones, senility, obesity, digestive disturbances, diabetes mellitus and tooth and gum problems. There are even foods specifically designed for long-coated breeds, as well as life-stage formulas. You can also choose from holistic diets that contain no artificial additives, and special diets for allergy sufferers.

Necessary nutrients

Generally, dogs are not difficult to feed, and they thrive on a diet not dissimilar to our own, albeit with a little more protein. Nearly all foods of animal origin, cereals, root vegetables and fats are easy for them to digest. The secret of correct feeding is to give your dog a balanced diet that supplies

Water is essential for life itself, and your dog should always have access to a fresh, clean supply. Refill the water bowl each day, and clean it regularly.

all the essential nutrients in the proper proportions. These nutrients are as follows:

Carbohydrates

Carbohydrates, in the form of cooked cereal starch, or sugar, can supply up to 70 per cent by weight of the dog's food (after deducting any water) or about two-thirds of the calories. Dog biscuits, pasta and rice are three useful energy foods for dogs; rice is a particularly useful foodstuff for dogs with an allergy to wheat.

Proteins

Proteins in meat and plants help to build body tissue, carry out 'repairs' and make hormones. The dry matter of dog food should contain at least 15 per cent protein, of which at least half should come from animal foods (meat and dairy products), or high-quality vegetable protein such as soya.

Minerals

Minerals are sometimes referred to as 'ash' on dog-food labels. The important ones are calcium and phosphorus. Calcium and phosphorus make up most of the mineral matter of bone and should be supplied at the rate of about 3 per cent calcium/ phosphorus in the diet; too much calcium in the diet, especially in large-breed puppies, can lead to skeletal abnormalities, while too much phosphorus (found in high meat and offal diets) can cause eclampsia in lactating bitches. Other essential minerals, such as zinc and copper, occur naturally in meat, cereals and other ingredients of a balanced diet.

Vitamins

Vitamin A (retinol) is essential for growth and vision, while B vitamins are important for the maintenance, in particular, of the central nervous system. Vitamin D helps the body produce calcium, essential for healthy

Some companies make canine birthday cakes specially prepared using suitable, healthy ingredients.

bones and teeth, as is phosphorus. Vitamin E (tocopherol) is vital for cell membranes. Since dogs can produce their own vitamin C (ascorbic acid), this does not need to be included in the diet.

Fat

Fat makes food tastier, but is actually only necessary as a source of the essential fatty acids (EFAs) that are vital for body health – they control water loss through the skin. A deficiency in EFAs can often result in problems such as reproductive, skin, coat and wound healing.

Fibre

A lack of fibre (roughage) in the diet can result – especially in elderly, inactive dogs – in constipation and other types of digestive problems cause by sluggish bowels. Fibre is supplied through the indigestible plant matter in foods such as cooked and raw vegetables and cereals.

Balancing act

It is important that the balance of nutrients fed to a dog is correct, because excesses can

DAILY FEEDING GUIDE

IDEAL WEIGHT OF ADULT DOG	AMOUNT OF FOOD
2kg (5lb)	110g–140g (4oz–5oz)
5kg (10lb)	200g–280g (7oz–10oz)
10kg (25lb)	400g–570g (14oz–1lb 4oz)
20kg (50lb)	680g–900g (1lb 8oz–2lb)
35kg (75lb)	900g–1.1kg (2lb–2lb 8oz)
45kg (100lb)	1.25–1.6kg (2lb 12oz–3lb 8oz)
70kg (150lb)	1.7–2.5kg (3lb 12oz–5lb 8oz)

cause as many health problems as deficiencies. If your dog receives more calories per day than his body needs, he will get fat. As in humans, obesity is responsible for such canine diseases as heart problems, joint ailments and a reduction in lung function. The safest and most effective way to meet canine nutrient requirements is to feed your dog on foods prepared by reputable manufactureres, as recommended on the labels.

How much should I feed to my dog?

This depends on your dog's size, daily activity level, age, individual nature and the temperature of his surroundings.

Young dogs and those being worked, or which are very active on a daily basis, may need more food (calories) per day than the average pet dog, whereas an old, inactive dog will require less.

Counting the calories

Energy is measured in units of heat called calories. In a healthy dog, the number of calories he requires balances with the number of calories that his body uses each day. If this balance is well maintained, the dog stays fit and healthy and his weight remains constant. An underfed dog gradually loses weight and condition as his body draws on the reserves of fat and lean body mass to make up the deficiencies in his diet.

The number of calories a dog needs per day depends on his size, life stage, level of activity and individuality. As an example, a small healthy adult dog with two hours of average activity a day requires anything between 125 and 700 calories per day depending on his size; a large dog will require from 1,400 calories per day, depending on size. Like us, all dogs are individuals with their own needs. Intake may also have to be adjusted in line with results.

Puppies need more calories in relation to their body weight because they are growing rapidly, they are more prone to heat loss due to their small size, and their energy requirements are higher. Lactating bitches need some 50 to 60 per cent more calories than norma, while highly active dogs need at least 40 per cent more calories than normal moderately active requirements.

Commercially prepared dog foods are available in (top to bottom) wet, semi-moist and dry varieties.

FOOD TYPES: AT-A-GLANCE GUIDE

FOOD TYPE	PROS	CONS
Wet/moist (canned)	• Extremely palatable. • Contains all the nutrients a dog needs. • Long storage time if unopened.	• Bulky to store and heavy to carry. • Fattening if too much is eaten. • Strong odour. • Not good for teeth. • Meat/other ingredient sources unidentifiable. • Contains many artificial additives. • Expensive. • Spoils quickly. • Can cause digestive upsets in some dogs.
Semi-moist (pouches/foil trays)	• Palatable. • Contains all the nutrients a dog needs. • Easier to store than cans.	• Fattening if too much is eaten. • Strong odour. • Not good for teeth. • Meat/other ingredient sources unidentifiable. • Very expensive. • Spoils quickly. • Contains man-made artificial additives.
Dry complete (packs)	• Economical. • Low odour. • Contains all the nutrients a dog needs. • Better for teeth due to abrasive action when fed dry. • Lighter to carry than cans. • Convenient to feed.	• Bulky to store. • Goes off if stored too long. • Not as palatable as canned/semi-moist. • High cereal content can cause problems for gluten-sensitive dogs.
Dry complementary (packs)	• Economical. • Low odour. • Good source of energy. • Most are supplemented with vitamins and minerals. • Better for teeth due to abrasive action when fed dry. • Lighter to carry than cans.	• Time-consuming to mix with protein-giving ingredients. • Spoils if stored too long. • Bulky to store.
Home-made diet (cooked and/or raw meat, table scraps, cereals, dairy products, fruit and vegetables)	• Economical. • Uses up waste food from the table, so environmentally friendly. • Raw crunchy vegetables, such as carrots, aid dental hygiene and provide a fresh source of nutrients. • Chewing raw meat helps clean the gums and teeth. • Sourced ingredients.	• Some essential nutrients may be lacking. • Fattening if too many table scraps are given. • Raw meat is likely to harbour parasites or harmful bacteria. • Raw meat spoils quickly. • Time-consuming sourcing and preparing ingredients. • Strong odour when cooking. • Bulky to store/refrigerate pre-prepared food.

Food types

Good quality proprietary food is the easiest to feed. It contains all the necessary nutrients in the correct proportions, including vitamins and minerals, often lacking from a home-made diet of fresh or cooked meat and table scraps. There are four forms of commercially prepared food to choose from.

Wet/moist (canned or pouch)

Canned food has a high water content, is available in a wide range of flavours and is usually the preferred choice of dogs.

Semi-moist (pouch)

Often containing vegetable protein, such as soya, this food type contains less water than canned, therefore keeps well in a bowl without drying out and losing texture.

Dry complete

Dry complete food contains minimal water and all the nutrients your dog needs. Some types are designed to be moistened with water before feeding, while other types can be fed as they are. Your dog will need plenty of water to drink in conjunction with them.

Dry complementary

Designed to be fed with canned, cooked or raw meat, this food usually comprises cereal meal or biscuits. Fed alone, it does not fulfil a dog's daily nutritional needs.

Check the label

Manufacturers' guidelines, as printed on food packs, are a good indicator of how much to feed daily, but remember all dogs are individuals and each has his own requirements. Decrease or increase your dog's daily intake of food depending on his condition and his daily level of activity.

Life-stage feeding

Different feeding regimes are appropriate for the various stages in a dog's life. (See chart below) As your dog gets older he needs fewer meals each day (see chart below).

Dietary extras

When on a commercially prepared diet, your dog should not need additional food supplements, comprising oils, minerals and vitamins, unless your vet advises otherwise. Overdosing your pet on nutrients can prove detrimental to his health.

LIFE-STAGE FEEDING

Puppies	Puppies usually stop drinking their mothers' milk and go on to solid food proper when they are 5–6 weeks old; gradual weaning starts around 3 weeks. Once fully weaned on to puppy food, they should be kept on this as it contains all the essential nutrients they need in a form that is easy for them to digest and utilize. Fed correctly at this age, they will be on course to grow into healthy and well-developed adults.
From weaning to 20 weeks	Puppies should receive three meals a day, plus an evening dish of milk.
From 20 to 30 weeks	Three meals a day.
From 30 weeks to 9 months	Two meals a day (depending on breed/growth rate).
From 9 months to 8 years	One or two meals a day.
From 8 years onwards (elderly)	One or two meals a day depending on your pet's condition and health.

When should I feed my dog?

Most owners feed either in the morning or the evening, and sometimes both, depending on their dog's age, needs or individual preference. Some dogs fare better with their daily ration split into two or even three meals, while others are happy to eat their daily allowance in one helping (providing it is safe for them to do so – see 'Eating habits' on page 24 – and never work a dog on a full stomach).

It is best not to feed adult dogs at the same times every day, as relying on a rigid routine can prove distressing for a dog whenever you are not able to feed him at the expected time. Not knowing when it will be fed also helps keep a dog food-orientated, which usually proves most helpful when training; it also discourages fussy eating.

Feeding guidelines

Here are some basic guidelines to follow:
• Place a feeding mat, or newspaper, under feeding bowls if your dog is a messy eater.
• It is best to introduce changes to diet gradually to avoid digestive upsets.
• Never give spiced food or that to which any alcohol has been added.
• To prevent choking, remove all bones from fresh meats and fish.
• Fresh, clean drinking water should always be available, whatever he is being fed.
• Make sure food and water bowls are always clean.
• Never allow your dog to eat chocolate intended for human consumption, as it is toxic for them.
• Consult your vet if your dog shows any reluctance to eat or drink.
• Discourage your dog begging at the table, and certainly don't give into it. Sometimes it can be hard to resist those pleading eyes, but you must for the sake of your dog's waistline and health.

FOOD HYGIENE

• Canned foods deteriorate quickly once opened, so refrigerate and use within 24 hours. To avoid tin contamination, decant leftover canned foods into ceramic, stainless steel or plastic food containers.
• Household disinfectants and detergents can taint food and water bowls and put your pet off using them, so it is preferable to use salt solution (1 teaspoon to half a litre/1 pint of water) or proprietary pet bowl cleaners, and then rinse thoroughly in clean water to clean and disinfect them. Clean bowls daily – your dog's good health depends on it.
• Wash pet feeding items separately from your own dishes and utensils.
• When feeding semi-moist food, reseal the packet to make it airtight in order to retain freshness and reduce moisture loss until the next mealtime.

To help establish hierarchy rules, always feed your new dog after the family has eaten and do not allow him to 'hound' you at the table.

A healthy environment

For your dog to be mentally and physically healthy, he must feel safe and secure in his environment. If you are to remain unworried and be able to enjoy your pet to the full, you must be positive that you are doing all you can to keep him happy and protected from harm. Fulfilling your dog's essential needs within his environment will help you both remain contented – and sane. As long as these needs are met, he will be a very happy dog.

Living accommodation

You should live in a house large enough to accommodate your family and your chosen size and type of dog, with plenty of space for everyone. Remember, you are buying a pet, not an accessory. It is no use thinking about a Great Dane, Afghan Hound, Border Collie, German Shepherd Dog or any other large working or herding breed if you live in a flat or small townhouse as these dogs don't thrive, mentally as well as physically, by being 'cooped up'. If you don't have a suitably sized garden in which to exercise him, then you must be prepared for two one-hour walks or so per day, with somewhere safe to exercise off-lead.

Similarly, if you live in the country and are looking for a companion for long walks, a Pekingese is not for you – they prefer the indoor, pampered life as the companion of a devoted owner.

If your home environment is not suited to the type of dog, then it can be a recipe for disaster. If you do your homework, however, and choose your dog well for the type of environment you can offer him, then you have the best chance of enjoying a match made in heaven.

The house proud must be prepared for extra work in keeping the home sweet-smelling and free of dog hairs and muddy paw prints. For minimal mess – and stress to all concerned – don't get a large, hairy, slobbery dog.

Home comforts

Important allowances for pet dogs include their own personal space comprising areas where they

Many people fancy a sporting dog, like this English Springer Spaniel, for a pet, but live to regret their choice if they cannot provide enough exercise and mental stimulation.

SAFE AND SECURE

Just like you, your dog needs to feel secure in his world to remain calm and contented. Providing adequately for your pet's essential needs, mentally and physically, is the first step towards achieving this ideal. A feeling of security is enhanced by respecting your dog's personal space. Providing safe places where your dog can rest without being bothered by anyone (especially children when the dog has had enough of play) or another animal, or simply watch the world go by from a safe vantage point, is paramount to your dog's emotional well-being. Just as we like to have time by ourselves for a while – to be able to relax, be alone with our thoughts, or to sleep undisturbed to recharge our batteries – so too do dogs. Just as we are likely to become irritable if our personal space and time is invaded, so too are dogs. So the rule is to let sleeping dogs lie!

A 'sanctuary' where your dog knows he can go to rest undisturbed is essential for his mental and physical well-being.

can rest undisturbed, toys that fulfil their hunting instincts through what we view as play, and sufficient food and water to satisfy their body needs (see pages 24–29).

As most people who keep dogs as pets want their animals to be close to them for the affection and company they provide, it stands to reason that the majority are kept in the home. To make your home as appealing as possible to your pet, meaning that the relationship between you both will be as successful and problem-free as possible, you must provide him with the facilities most important to him.

Your temperament

Another consideration is how you relate to your dog. Whatever dog you choose, he will sense your emotions, so a stressed owner is likely to end up with a stressed pet. Dogs respond best to calm, consistent handling. Shouting at or hitting him will confuse and frighten him resulting in behaviour problems in the future.

A good owner is patient and controlled enough not to become angry at a dog if he does something you perceive as wrong. If he does something inappropriate as far as you are concerned, then you have not trained him or catered for his needs adequately. Look at what may have caused the problem, and then rectify it. Is he receiving enough attention, exercise and so on? Find the root cause of the problem and you are halfway to finding the solution.

BE SAFE, NOT SORRY

Not taking out appropriate insurance when you get a dog could prove false economy. It could mean being faced with a massive veterinary bill if your dog needs extensive treatment, while a lawsuit against you for personal or property damage caused by your dog could leave you facing financial ruin. Shop around for the best insurance deal and ask your local vet for any recommendations; then remember to read the small print on policy proposals.

Some dogs dislike being left at home alone while their owners are out at work, and suffer separation anxiety.

BOREDOM BEATERS

A filled Kong toy will help keep your dog occupied when you are not there. You can also use it to distract him when necessary.

1 *Fill the Kong with soft cheese or peanut butter. Push biscuit treats down into the soft filling.*

2 *Seal in the filling by smoothing it with a knife. Give the toy to your dog to enjoy!*

Your lifestyle

If you work all day, you should consider getting a dog that will not mind spending large periods of time on his own. (This is likely to be an adult, since it is not fair to leave puppies on their own for any length of time). Alternatively, you could arrange to have someone come and see to the dog at least once during your absence and let him out to relieve himself.

If you get a puppy, the first couple of months are going to be particularly time-consuming – you will need to spend time on house training and basic obedience training. Later, you will need to allow at least two hours every day for care and exercise. Are you able to devote this essential time to exercise, train and play

with a dog? If not, perhaps you should rethink your reasons for getting one.

Playtime

Establishing certain times when you can devote attention to your dog will soon become a regular routine he looks forward to, and make his attention-seeking a thing of the past. To make this quality time interesting and more fulfilling for both of you, invest in a selection of toys that your pet finds entertaining, and choose toys according to his perceived value of them; 'low-value' toys can be given for everyday use, while 'high-value' toys are extremely useful when training.

A suitably-sized ball for your dog to chase and retrieve and an activity toy (such as a puzzle feeder, or stuffed Kong – see the panel above for how to do this) to keep him occupied will do fine to start with. Home-

Even if you have more than one dog, they will be happier for spending time interacting with you.

made toys can also include cardboard boxes filled with scrunched-up newspaper in which toys or food treats are hidden, while games you can play with your dog include hiding toys or treats around the house for him to find.

Should you wish to purchase a selection of low-value and high-value toys, there is a vast range specially designed for dogs available in pet stores to suit all budgets and types of dog. Bear in mind that strong-jawed dogs, such as Bull Terriers and Schnauzers, soon destroy toys, so choose those that are durable (unless you have an unlimited budget). Do not use brittle sticks as they can damage the mouth.

Interaction

Different dogs require different degrees of social contact with their owners and others of their own kind. Some will be more independent and aloof than their owners wish, while others need plenty of attention in order to thrive. Dogs that actively seek out human company show signs of distress if they cannot get enough.

Dogs that have a low need for social contact may learn to tolerate their owners' attention, but never seem to really enjoy it, so this desire must be recognized and accepted. For a person who requires an openly affectionate canine companion, this can be disappointing, so it pays to research which breeds would be best suited.

Being social creatures, most dogs appreciate the company of their own kind on a regular basis to enact natural

ROUGH PLAY

Be aware that rough play can lead to your dog becoming confused as to what behaviour is acceptable and what is not. For example, if you decide to get down on the floor and play-wrestle with the dog, then it is likely that he will try to dominate the situation. This often gets out of hand; his natural instincts come to the fore and this can result in injury to a member of the family, often with disastrous consequences for all concerned.

If this happens, it is usually the dog that gets the blame, yet it is not his fault, but rather that of human failure to understand the behavioural boundaries between the two species. This is why it is so important to teach children, being more impulsive and less aware of what could happen, how to behave around pets of any kind. On this theme, do advise visitors of how to behave around your dog if you feel that their behaviour is not appropriate in the circumstances – for both their own and your pet's sake. If you are worried, put your dog in the garden.

Being with members of their own species is important to most dogs, so they should be allowed the opportunity to socialize on a regular basis.

interaction. However many of the 'fighting' breeds simply do not get on amicably with strange dogs (males and females alike), or indeed even with people, so beware of this when taking them out for walks; for safety's sake; such dogs should be muzzled when in public places, and in some countries this is, in fact, a legal requirement.

If you have a dog that simply does not get on with other dogs – and some don't – then again extreme caution should be taken when they are exercised in public places.

Environmental harmony

There are a couple of things to consider in order to achieve this ideal. The first is your dog's safety inside the house, in the garden and beyond, and the second is maintaining good relations with your neighbours.

Indoor safety

Although you think your home may be safe for your dog, there are in fact a number of potential hazards you need to be aware of for your pet's well-being.

• **Cleaning fluids and detergents** Make sure your dog does not have access to them.
• **Powder carpet fresheners** these may burn the pads of a dog's feet, as well as cause skin and respiratory problems.
• **Electric leads** Many puppies love to chew them, and young curious dogs may play with them. Install a safety trip mechanism.
• **Sewing materials and stationery** Keep needles, thread, pins, buttons, rubber bands, paper clips, etc., under lock and key.
• **Human medicines** Always keep these locked away.
• **Hot water** Especially in the bath. For both human and animal safety run the cold water first.
• **Noise** from the television, radio or sound system – a dog's hearing is highly sensitive.

Outdoor safety

Outdoor hazards include vehicular traffic, harassment from other dogs and humans, poisoning from harmful substances and poisonous creatures, and from contracting diseases from other dogs.

• **Garden/yard security** Make sure your fence is dog-proof so that your pet cannot escape. Inspect fencing daily and secure any holes in hedging or fencing immediately. Some dogs are excellent athletes and can scale a 2m (6ft) fence with no problem, especially entire dogs keen to find a mate, so ensure your boundary enclosure is suitable for the type and character of dog you own.

• **Poisons** Keep garden chemicals (such as weedkillers and slug pellets) safely locked away where your dog cannot gain access to them. If you service the car, clean up any spilt antifreeze and oil; dogs find antifreeze appetizing and will lick it, while oil on fur or paws can result in poisoning if it is ingested when the dog grooms himself. Most dogs will instinctively avoid poisonous plants, both indoor and outdoor (such as laburnum and poinsettia), but puppies – being interested in everything – can occasionally fall victim to them. If you are worried about this danger then, if possible, remove any plants that may prove fatal if eaten by dogs – your vet can advise on the worst offenders.

Dogs can also suffer poisoning from eating contaminated food they have found, such as poisoned vermin carcasses.

• **Toad poisoning** Dogs do tend to investigate frogs and toads, and catch the occasional one before they know any better. Toads emit a vile-tasting, sometimes toxic, substance when under threat. Dogs react to this by shaking their heads frantically, salivating profusely and pawing at their mouth in an effort to rid themselves of the nasty, irritating substance. If you suspect toxic toad poisoning, consult your local vet immediately.

• **Snake bites** Consult your vet immediately if you suspect your dog has been bitten by a poisonous snake.

For your dog's own safety, keep waste bins out of his reach.

Bringing your dog home

So that bringing your new pet home runs comfortably and smoothly, and is free of stress for all concerned, you must prepare for the big event. It is important to establish care rules and routine for all the family in advance of the big day when you will collect your dog. Setting a date well in advance will also give you time to get all the necessary items ready.

Getting him adjusted

For puppies, take a week or so off, as a young puppy will need feeding and letting out to relieve himself more often than an adult. Over this period, gradually train the puppy to wait a little longer between toilet times (adjusting feeding times gently, since puppies usually want to go after eating). Slowly leave him longer and longer without your attention, or presence, restricted to an area of the house where he can do little damage and which is safe for him, to accustom him to being left on his own. Arrange for someone to come in and see to the puppy at least once during the day while you are out until he is older and can cope better mentally and physically with your prolonged absences.

If your new dog is an adult, collect him in the middle of a weekend so you have just one day before everyone goes out to work or school and the everyday routine begins. If you spend a week at home, he will get used to having you around all the time and find it difficult to cope when normal routines resume.

Pre-arrival preparations

A couple of days before you collect a puppy, take his new bedding to the breeder so he can use it there. This is so that the puppy's own smell, or that of his mother and litter mates, will transfer to the bedding and make him feel more at home in his new environment.

Buy the equipment you will need (see pages 20–23), in particular a crate or sturdy carrier. Ask the breeder or owner what food the puppy is used to, so that you can get some, and how much he is being fed and how

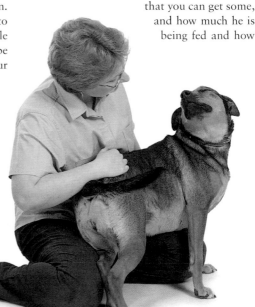

Let a new dog come to you when he is ready to do so – don't try to force him into interaction or you may frighten him.

It's important that you put your new dog's bed in a place where he can rest undisturbed yet not feel excluded from the family group.

often. When you collect him, line the carrier or crate with the bedding, put the puppy in and shut the door securely. Make sure you have all the paperwork from the former owner (receipt, pedigree papers, registration and ownership transfer documents and vaccination certificate) before setting off.

For an adult dog, you will need a crate, travel harness (if he is used to wearing one) or a dog grille to enclose him safely for his journey home.

Travelling home

Secure the carrier either on a seat with a seat belt, in the back of an estate vehicle, or in the footwell on the floor; a crate or travel harness should be placed in the rear of the car (never in an enclosed boot or trunk). The inside of the vehicle should be at a moderate temperature with sufficient airflow; too much heat can be fatal. Offer water in a bowl at regular intervals if you are travelling any distance. Even if your dog protests, do not be tempted to let him out; talk to him to reassure him. Covering the crate with a blanket may help calm an excitable, barking dog.

On arrival home

Take the dog home and walk him in the garden. Let him off the lead to run around and explore, then take him inside, so he can explore the house. Make sure the family do not fuss him and that children behave quietly and gently – do not let them handle him too much until he has got used to them.

Next, take him for a walk, or let him into the garden again and play a game with him, if appropriate, to begin the bonding process. After that, encourage him to rest on his bed for a while, leaving him undisturbed. Learning where his rest area is, and that he will be left in peace there, will help him settle. See pages 50–51 for detailed information on socializing your new pet with other animals.

Settling in

While a puppy usually settles in very quickly and adapts to your routine well, an adult dog often takes longer. He will feel displaced and unsettled for a while, and you should give him the time and space he needs to adjust. Try to be sympathetic to how your puppy feels, but do not allow any bad habits to form.

When taking your new dog or pup for a walk, keep him on the leash until you are confident he will come back immediately when called. A useful tip is to carry really smelly and tasty treats in your pocket. Let him sniff them, see where they are kept, and give him one every now and then, particularly when you feel his attention wandering away from you.

CANINE BEHAVIOUR

Many dogs are treated badly or inappropriately simply because their owners are ignorant of what their pets are telling them. Dogs have a language all of their own, but, if we observe them carefully, we can build up a detailed picture of their body language and actions that helps us guess how they might be feeling, what they want from us and what they need. By making an effort to learn what your dog is saying to you, you will understand him better and therefore be able to give him an improved quality of life.

Body language

Dogs employ a vast range of facial expressions, vocal sounds and body postures in order to communicate. Many owners talk to their dogs, and sometimes the two parties appear to understand each other. Dogs possess a large universal vocabulary, and some people have attempted to translate what they are saying.

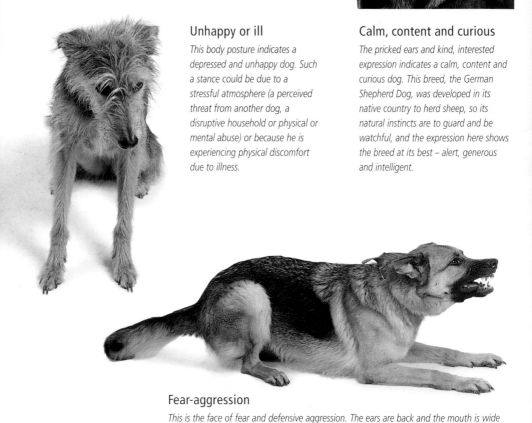

Unhappy or ill

This body posture indicates a depressed and unhappy dog. Such a stance could be due to a stressful atmosphere (a perceived threat from another dog, a disruptive household or physical or mental abuse) or because he is experiencing physical discomfort due to illness.

Calm, content and curious

The pricked ears and kind, interested expression indicates a calm, content and curious dog. This breed, the German Shepherd Dog, was developed in its native country to herd sheep, so its natural instincts are to guard and be watchful, and the expression here shows the breed at its best – alert, generous and intelligent.

Fear-aggression

This is the face of fear and defensive aggression. The ears are back and the mouth is wide with worry. However, the lips are drawn up slightly to expose the teeth, the head is up ready to bite and the eyes are fixed on the antagonist so that further aggressive action can be taken if necessary. This face is accompanied by a series of explosive barks designed to make the aggressor move away.

Frightened

A frightened dog will pull away from whatever it is that has worried him: the tail and ears are tucked well out of harm's way in case of attack, eyes are fixed on whatever is scaring him in case he needs to flee quickly, and the whites of the eyes show, indicating that the eyes are wide open to gather more information. The heart will be racing and body preparing itself for a fast getaway.

Uneasy

This dog's body stance and posture show that he is scared and very uneasy, with nowhere to hide or feel really safe. He is waiting miserably for better options to become available, his ears lifted to alert him to the tiniest sound indicating what is to happen next.

Playful

This is the signal that says 'I would like to play with you'. Dogs will give this signal to humans as well as other dogs and animals. This pose will be held for a few seconds, with the tail beating furiously, before the dog jumps up and runs off, looking over his shoulder to see if his invitation to chase has been successful. Many dogs do this as a greeting to show that a person they know is coming near.

Aggressive

This is a deliberate display of strength, and the 'adversary' is being given the chance to back down, but any retreat must be slow and obvious to avoid an attack. This expression is designed to show the dog's impressive weaponry – his teeth. The lips are drawn up as far as they will go.

Barking and howling

Barking is the dog's way of speaking and is used to sound an alarm and warn other pack members (human or animal) of intruders, as an effective way of warning off potential foes, and also to indicate a state of high excitement, such as during play. Howling is a good way to communicate with others who are far away. If separated from the pack (human or other dogs), howling and waiting for others to respond helps the lost one to know in which direction to travel to rejoin them.

Yawning and licking lips

Yawning and flicking their tongue in and out is often one of the first signs that your dog is uneasy about a situation. He may be in conflict within himself, trying to decide whether to move away, or he could be signalling to you that he is not happy about something. Humans frequently mistakenly think the dog is tired and take no notice of this important signal.

Listening

Cocking the head on one side is a way of turning the ears to better pinpoint the direction and source from which a sound is coming.

Wary

This is not a good way to greet an unfamiliar dog. Dogs, especially those that have been ill treated in the past, find this kind of approach worrying and try to shrink away from the 'threat', with their ears back (to protect them in case of attack), eyes wide open (to see the threat better) and their tail tucked between their legs (to keep it out of harm's way). Putting your hands towards and making eye contact with an unknown dog may well be perceived as a potential attack.

Submissive 'grinning'

A submissive 'grin' like this is often misinterpreted by humans, who think the dog is being aggressive. In reality, these 'grins' are similar to a human smile and are often shown when the dog is greeting people he knows or when he is being admonished. These 'grins' are usually reserved for humans rather than other dogs, and the propensity to show them seems to be inherited and to run in families.

OBSESSIVE BEHAVIOUR

Also known as a 'stereotypy', a dog that displays obsessive behaviour does so because the habit has become ingrained – a good example of this is a zoo animal pacing or rocking backwards and forwards. This gives them something to do and some kind of comfort. In dogs, an example of stereotypical behaviour is chasing their tails, and they become oblivious to everything around them as they circle and spin. Sometimes they catch it and make it bleed, but the important part to them is the chase – even if their tail is amputated, they will continue to pursue the stump. Providing a more stimulating environment and more games with toys can provide the dog with a more fulfilling life, negating the need for them to engage in obsessive behaviours. Causes of stereotypical behaviour include:

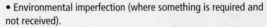

• Being in a regularly frightening situation (such as in an abusive environment).
• Frustration.
• Anticipation (for example, at feeding or exercise times).
• A mismatch between the environment and the dog.
• Environmental imperfection (where something is required and not received).
• The dog not understanding what is required of him.
• Isolation (lack of contact with humans or other animals).

Submission

Rolling on the back, exposing the belly and leaving himself vulnerable displays a dog's acceptance of a higher-ranking individual. This strategic positioning is a good one to get the dog out of a situation in which he would otherwise receive punishment.

The wolf in your home

Wolves, the ancestors of our pet dogs, are social animals. Humans have taken this trait and bred selectively over many generations so that the dogs we have in our homes are generally sociable and loyal. However, it must never be forgotten that dogs evolved as pack animals that had to compete with others and kill prey to survive, and these traits are still there beneath the surface of domesticity.

Where dogs came from

Dogs were in existence before the earliest human. According to fossil evolution, the origins of our dogs can be traced back about 40 million years to a small carnivorous mammal called Miacis. This tiny weasel-like creature gradually evolved to produce, some 10 million years ago, the forerunners of present-day canids, called Cynodesmus and Tomoritus. From them, the evolution of the canid line continued up to about 10,000–12,000 years ago when wolves – along with foxes, jackals and coyotes – appeared in the form they are today. Today's dog is derived from four types of wolf (*Canis lupus*): the northern grey wolf, the pale-footed Asian wolf, the small desert wolf of Arabia and the woolly-coated wolf of Tibet and northern India.

Modern dogs

Domestication occurred when humans as we know them came on the scene. However, 'modern' man's predecessors had already been co-existing with dog-like creatures for thousands of years. Various archaeological finds around the world support the theory that domestication probably began around 10,000–12,000 years ago in different parts of the globe rather than in one place.

The first domesticated dogs

Several theories exist as to how dogs were first domesticated in response to human social and work needs.

Hunting help

The first theory is that dogs were originally used by humans to help with hunting, in that the humans would scare off wolves from their kills and scavenge the remains. It is thought that, perhaps, by means of training orphaned wolf cubs, humans might have begun to employ wolves' hunting skills more directly.

Owner beware – even the smallest, cutest dog is a wolf in disguise, retaining the same instincts.

Food source

A second theory, though unlikely, is that humans hunted wolves for food and, in times of plenty, took back orphaned cubs as children's playthings.

Companion pets

A third theory is that, right from the start, dogs were pets or companions rather than a food source or working animals. Children might have reared orphaned wolfcubs as pets, with perhaps the cubs later utilized as working animals.

Guard dogs

The fourth theory is that early domestic dogs were used as guards rather than hunters, because their superior hearing and smell would allow them to notice danger before humans did. This may have extended to use with flocks of sheep and cattle.

Mutual benefits

A fifth theory is that humans did not actively domesticate the dog, but that a relationship developed between them to their mutual advantage. Dogs hung around settlements scavenging for food humans had discarded, as well as hunting rats and other species that lived on grain stored by humans. The tamer dogs that were thought useful in keeping down vermin, may have been then befriended by humans.

Living with man

Cave drawings discovered in the Pyrenees from the Upper Palaeolithic period (some 12,000–10,000 years ago) show archers and dogs co-operating in a hunt. The dogs are lightly built and long-legged, with pricked ears and pointed muzzles, very like the wolves that inhabited southern Europe, but with differences that show that humans were beginning to select the 'dogs' best suited to their purpose.

Trained sheepdogs are highly prized for their skills, both practically and in competitions.

Around 5,000 years ago, humans were beginning to settle and farm the land. This led to the development of types of dog suited to various tasks, such as herding and guarding, and not just exclusively for hunting. As humans became more prosperous, they could afford to keep dogs simply as pets and companions. Humans learned to breed dogs of all sizes and shapes for a wide variety of tasks – from the huge Mastiff-like war dogs of the Babylonian Empire to the fleet-footed hunting hounds bred by the Assyrians.

In more recent times, dogs have been used to accompany carriages, hunt, provide 'entertainment' fighting pits for gamblers, be pampered lap dogs and drag heavy loads such as sleds.

Gradually, throughout the twentieth century, many of the traditional canine uses were phased out, to be replaced with nothing more than humans' desire to keep dogs as pets, and in working roles of helpers for less able people and in law enforcement. In many ways, dogs continue to contribute to the quality of our lives.

Normal behaviour

Dogs display a number of traits that humans find annoying, strange or even disgusting (eating faeces is a prime example). Yet dogs do what they do for a reason. As far as they are concerned, they are doing nothing wrong, and they become confused when we scold them. Knowing why dogs do certain things will enable you to cope better with them as they occur.

Vocal communication

Compared to humans, dogs have a limited ability to communicate using sound and tend to rely more on body language to get their message across. The range of sounds they produce tends to be used to back up their body language rather than in isolation. Howling and growling are the least common sounds, but barking is used frequently, often in different ways to convey different meanings. These can range from guarding barks to those designed to get attention, or barking can be used just to let off steam when excited or frustrated.

Barking to get attention is common in pampered small dogs when they feel their owners are ignoring them.

Guarding and possession

Natural instinct dictates that to let another take away food will result in hunger. This principle sometimes gets transferred to toys and other items a dog possesses; to give them up is a sign of weakness. Guarding food or a toy, by growling or snapping at anyone who approaches, is a dog's way of saying 'this is mine and you are not having it'. However, this line of defence is inappropriate in a human environment. In pet dogs, not letting go of something must be discouraged from an early age, otherwise aggression problems may later result. It is perfectly fine to let a non-aggressive or non-possessive dog occasionally win the toy in a game to keep his play motivation high, but this should be the exception, not the rule.

Hierarchical behaviour patterns

A pet dog often instinctively wants to become 'top dog' in a household 'pack'. This is because the strongest animals get the best food, the most comfortable sleeping places and the chance to breed and pass on their genes to the next generation. Dogs in a wild pack live in a social hierarchy. Good leaders look after the pack, making sure they are well fed and are comfortable. They are uncompromising and tough when necessary to maintain authority. They have sufficient strength to earn respect without constantly harassing or bullying the pack to stay in control.

In domestic circumstances, you must remember that you are the leader and your dog is the lower-status pack member. If the status alters, you will certainly have problems in controlling your dog's behaviour. However, if this happens, all is not lost: the hierarchy in a wild dog pack is not fixed and will change if circumstances alter. Therefore, there is hope for humans whose dog has taken control of them (see pages 58–59, Handling Dogs).

Chase drive

Humans have domesticated dogs and selectively bred them until they no longer resemble their wild ancestors, but they still retain many of the characteristics that make them efficient hunters. The hunting sequence can be broken down into components – scent-trail, watch, stalk, chase, grab, bite, shake, kill, consume – all of which can be seen in our own docile pets.

Different breeds of dog have been bred to exploit different elements of the hunting sequence: hounds are bred to track and trail, herding dogs to chase and terriers to catch and kill. If this strong desire to chase things is not channelled into acceptable working behaviour or games with toys, dogs can pick up bad habits and get into trouble for carrying out inappropriate chases, such as pursuing other animals, cars, joggers or cyclists.

Information gathering

Your dog can find out a lot by stopping and sniffing the urine and faeces left by other dogs. Although this procedure may be repellent to humans, your dog uses it to find who was recently in the area, just as we find out what is happening by using our primary sense of sight. Scents linger for some time and, to a dog, sniffing is like watching a video of all the things that may have happened in that place recently.

Urinating against posts and defecating on or next to another dog's motions is a highly effective 'messaging service'. The scent left behind is their 'calling card'.

TAIL-WAGGING EXPLAINED

A wagging tail does not always indicate a friendly and happy dog. You have to take into account the rest of his body language before deciding whether he is a friend or a foe. Wagging a raised, stiff tail implies tension and potential aggression, while wagging a low tail, possibly between his legs, indicates a submissive or fearful dog. Energetically wagging at half-mast is usually a good sign as, generally, it means the dog is neither tense nor depressed. As well as the wag, look at the dog's hackles (the top of the shoulder, just behind the neck), his body stance and facial expressions. If his hackles are raised (the hair will be stood up and bushed out), he is stiff-legged and has a fixed-eye expression, then this indicates to a person, or another animal, that the dog is on his guard and ready to attack if he deems it necessary. If the wagging tail comes complete with a relaxed body stance, 'smiley' face and lolling ears, then the dog is not looking for confrontation, but rather to play or receive some attention.

In 'squaring up', the dog on the left is displaying the attitude of being 'armed to attack'; his hackles are raised, his teeth are bared and his body stance tense.

Aggression

Dogs will only attack with intent if absolutely crucial for their own well-being: in the wild, harming another pack member is only ever done as a last resort, because having an incapacitated dog means that there is one fewer to go out to find food and to guard the group as a whole.

Dogs who sleep with their eyes closed and body totally relaxed indicate they feel safe in their surroundings.

Interaction with others

A dog that presents no threat to humans and other animals tends either to ignore them completely, as if they were not there, or to greet them with his body totally relaxed and not tense. His tail will wag in a wide sweeping movement from side to side, and his facial expression will be one of a happy, silly 'grin', or of calm contentment (see page 40). Licking whoever he is greeting is an appeasement gesture that the dog uses to signal that he is no threat. He does this in the hope that whoever it is won't attack him.

Sleeping

Dogs spend quite a lot of time sleeping, especially as they get older, but do not necessarily sleep all night as we generally expect them to. Providing puppies and young dogs with something to do when they wake up (such as leaving them toys to play with) can help prevent you suffering disturbed sleep. Many dogs prefer to sleep underneath some sort of protection, such as a table or bed, or behind a sofa. This could be linked to the trait of 'going to ground' in times of danger when puppies were raised in dens.

Playing

Generally, dogs are highly social creatures and love nothing more than the company of other dogs and to play silly games with them. However, whether or not two dogs will get on depends on how compatible their personalities are and how they are introduced.

Some dogs are shy and worried about others, whereas some are outgoing and are happy to meet as many other dogs as possible. As with people, some dogs are good at communication, but others often get into fights and squabbles because of confusion over their intentions. Signalling

Licking a person's face has its origins in the behaviour of puppies in the wild who licked the mouths of adult dogs returning to the nest to get them to regurgitate the food they were carrying in their stomachs.

and body language play a large part in these encounters, and indicate how well a dog has been socialized with other dogs during and since puppyhood.

Personal hygiene

Few owners enjoy the sight of a dog using his tongue to clean his private places, but it is essential to realize that this is a necessary part of his personal hygiene. Most dogs are very efficient at keeping themselves clean without any help from humans, apart from those with gastric ailments resulting in diarrhoea (especially longhaired dogs), obese dogs who cannot reach their nether regions and older dogs who are not very flexible. It is important that you attend to these dogs' hygiene needs and wash their anal and genital areas, especially in hot weather when there are lots of flies about.

Scavenging

Most pet dogs get food handed to them at least once a day and never have to find their own food. Humans often feel that, because of this, there is no need for dogs to hunt or scavenge, and often punish them for doing so. However, until we breed dogs that have very little remaining of the genetics of their ancestors, dogs will continue to have the drives and desires that allowed their predecessors to acquire enough to eat. Dogs can be trained not to raid the kitchen bin; in the case of a confirmed scavenger, however, the simplest thing to do is to make sure the bin is not kept where he has access to it.

Five steps to successful integration

1 Learn how to interpret your dog's body language, and so recognize his state of mind; remember that tail-wagging does not always mean a dog is friendly.

2 A 'tense' body indicates uncertainty, fear or potential aggression, while a 'soft' body stance and movement denotes a relaxed, happy dog.

3 Remember how a dog's natural instincts dictate his behaviour, and learn how to work with this.

4 Find out the different breeds' inherent traits and use this knowledge to determine your ideal canine companion.

5 Remember not to get cross with your dog, but simply prevent him from doing the things that could be ultimately harmful to him by distracting him with a game or toy.

Socializing

Dogs must be well socialized from a very early age if they are to accept humans, the domestic environment in which they live and other dogs and animals without any kinds of problem behaviour occurring.

Social contact

Dogs are social creatures. Different breeds of dog enjoy the company of people and other animals to different extents, but all like to live their lives in a pack with others, whether human or canine. If denied social contact, they can become badly behaved or depressed. An undersocialized dog can be difficult to live with, handle and control, and should be properly socialized for the safety and contentment of all concerned.

Teach children to give the dog treats, both by hand and also by adding them to his dish while he is eating a meal.

Human contact

Dogs need to be taught to behave well around all humans. Examples of these include the following:
• Wheelchair users, people with walking sticks or crutches and the elderly.
• Babies, toddlers, timid people and people who are not comfortable around dogs.
• Energetic and noisy children and adults.
• Joggers, cyclists, rollerbladers, skateboarders and people pushing prams.
• People with beards, unusual hairstyles, spectacles, headgear, uniforms or umbrellas.

Delivery people

Many dogs have a particular problem with delivery people, because of territorial aggression (a form of fear aggression).

Delivery people come to his territory, where he is most confident, and then, from the dog's point of view, go as soon as they are barked at, so the barking has worked.

To prevent aggression towards delivery people, make a point of introducing your dog to them, and getting them to give him treats or even throwing a toy for him, so that he views them as rewarding and so welcomes them.

Different environments

Things that are normal to us in our everyday environment both inside and outside the home can be confusing, even frightening, to a dog if he has not been properly introduced to and socialized with them. Items such as a vacuum cleaner, slippery floors, stairs, traffic, hair-drier, the television and washing machine can all be sources of mental distress to a dog.

Get your dog used to such things gradually but persistently, using lots of treats and games so that he views them as rewarding experiences. If your dog has grown up in a busy household, then he is more likely to view household appliances with indifference, but an older dog unused to them needs careful introductions in short training sessions so as not to daunt him.

How to socialize your dog

Socialize your dog at his own pace. Rushing this process can result in him becoming nervous and timid, even aggressive, or it could make formed behaviour problems worse, rather than alleviating them. Make introductions to new experiences short and sweet so that your dog views them as good things. Here are some examples.

Going to the vet

Arrange to take your dog just for gentle handling and a treat from your vet, so that he doesn't associate going to the vet with purely unpleasant experiences.

Car travel

Feed your dog in the car, or have games in it with the doors open (parked in a safe, off-road spot) to begin with, so that your dog sees the car as a nice thing to be in. Then make initial journeys very short, ending with going for an enjoyable walk before returning home.

Staying in boarding kennels

Arrange to take your dog to the kennels to meet the staff and to play games with him there. Then take him again another day and leave him for an hour or so, with a toy and his bed for familiarity, so that he learns that you will come back for him. Progress to a day, and then an overnight stay.

Being groomed

Accustom your dog to being regularly groomed by you and other family members, and friends if possible, so that if he needs to go to a grooming parlour and be groomed by strangers it won't be so much of a problem for him. Take him to the parlour for an initial visit to meet the staff, then when he goes for the real thing he is more likely to feel comfortable about it. Some parlours don't mind you staying while your dog is groomed, but some dogs are better behaved when their owners are not there.

Taking your dog to introduction classes where he can socialize with other humans and dogs will help teach him how to behave appropriately in the company of others.

Socialization

Use this chart to monitor your dog's socialization progress. You can customize the chart as regards your dog's age as necessary, and add features such as agility classes, dustcarts, trains, buses, large vehicles, ice cream vans, tractors or horse riders. Put a tick in the box for each example as your pet is introduced to each element – entering as many ticks per box as possible (indicating how many encounters your dog has had) – and expanding on his reaction, and if anything needs to be worked on further, in a diary kept for the purpose. This way you can keep an accurate track of your dog's progress. Take care not to overwhelm your pet; take things at his pace. Some areas may need more acclimatization than others, so be prepared for this – but remember that time and patience really do work wonders.

Remember that it is essential your dog sees these encounters as good and not bad ones, otherwise they could scare him and make him resistant to coping with them in a positive way, so ensure each meeting is made as pleasant for him as possible. The use of food or toy rewards are good ways of ensuring he views each encounter as rewarding, and therefore non-threatening.

SOCIALIZATION PROGRAMME

AGE	6–7 weeks	7–8 weeks
Adults		
Young adults		
Middle-aged adults		
Elderly people		
Disabled/infirm		
Loud, confident people		
Shy, timid people		
Delivery people		
Joggers		
People wearing uniforms		
People wearing hats		
People with beards		
People wearing glasses		
People wearing helmets		
Children		
Babies		
Toddlers		
Juniors		
Teenagers		
Other animals		
Dogs – adults		
Dogs – puppies		
Cats		
Small pets		
Livestock		
Horses		
Environments		
Friend's house		
Shopping centre		
Park		
Outside a school		
Outside a children's play area		
Country walks		
Other		
Bicycles		
Motorbikes		
Traffic		

8–9 weeks	9–10 weeks	10–11 weeks	11–12 weeks	3–6 months	6–10 months

Should I get a second dog?

You want to get a second dog or puppy to provide your existing pet with a friend and company when you are out. This might seem like a good idea initially, but will the reality be as rewarding as the concept? Before going ahead and getting another dog, ask yourself the following questions.

Compatibility

While most dogs are highly social animals, introducing a resident dog to a newcomer is not always as easy as you might imagine it to be. So, it is important to consider your existing dog's temperament before getting another one. Some breeds do not co-exist well with other dogs, so this is another consideration – see pages 12–19 for information on different breed and type characteristics.

Introducing a second dog

Dogs do not live by the same code of conduct that humans do, so, instead of smiling and shaking hands on first meeting, they may well swear at each other and have a punch-up. As this would not start the relationship off on the right footing, careful introductions are essential so that this situation does not occur.

Bonding

Some dogs bond so closely that the owner is left out of the equation. To avoid this happening, you will need to separate the dogs if they are left alone for any length of time, either during the day while you are at work, or at night. Do this by means of a mesh partition or a stair gate so they can

Two dogs that get on well together enjoy a wonderful friendship – and you get twice the pleasure.

Usually, introductions between a new dog and the existing one go smoothly, with the new dog acting, and being treated like, a visitor.

still keep each other company, but can't play together unless you are there to supervise them. So that the dogs won't feel entirely 'abandoned' during the day, give them something to occupy their time alone such as activity toys, or have someone come in to give them attention, to take them for a walk, and just to let them outside to relieve themselves. It is also a good idea to regularly take each dog out separately, so that you can devote your attention to each one singly. The new dog will learn to be confident when out alone, and not to rely on the other dog for support.

BRINGING YOUR NEW PET HOME

DO	DON'T
• Follow the steps given in 'Socializing' on pages 50–53 and in 'Bringing your dog home' on pages 36–37.	• Interfere in the natural process of the dogs sorting out the hierarchy between themselves in the first couple of weeks – unless they actually begin to fight. If it becomes obvious that the new dog has taken control, you will have to reinforce his rank by putting the new dog first in everything instead.
• Expect integration to take some time.	
• Allow the dogs to investigate each other at their own pace without distractions.	
• Feed the dogs separately to begin with.	
• Give the new dog his own bed and toys to minimize disagreements over possessions.	• Aggravate a situation between the dogs during the settling-in period; for example, shut them in separate rooms to fuss and give them treats.
• Initially, reinforce the existing dog's position as leader of the canine 'pack' by favouring him first when playing, feeding, giving attention and allowing him to go through doorways first.	• Lift (in the case of small dogs) one dog above the other; by doing so, you will give the underdog a height advantage that can trigger the top dog into aggression.
	• Leave the dogs together until you are certain they have become friends.

CARING FOR A DOG

Part of the attraction of owning one of these wonderful creatures is the interaction many owners enjoy in keeping their dog happy and healthy. There are many aspects to dog care and management, and it is extremely satisfying to know that you are paying meticulous attention to all the needs of the animal in your care. For many people, the daily routine involved in looking after a dog, from preparing his dinner to enjoying a romp in the countryside, is very fulfilling, and the loyal and unwavering affection received in return supremely rewarding.

Handling dogs

The manner in which you handle and interact with your dog will affect his behaviour and reactions towards you. In situations where there is tension in the air, they hear loud or raised voices, are touched roughly or are grabbed at suddenly, dogs feel threatened and insecure.

Physical communication

Most pet dogs learn to enjoy being fussed and stroked from an early age and appreciate being touched – particularly on the back, chest and sides, which are 'safe' areas. Areas that a dog will instinctively be wary about having touched are his eyes, mouth, paws, ears, tummy, tail and anal area. However, it is important to accustom your dog to having these areas touched without a fuss, in case they need grooming or veterinary attention.

Dogs threaten each other by staring and they learn quickly to take avoiding action if this happens, rather than risk the aggression that would otherwise accompany the staring. Humans tend to gaze lovingly at their pet, so it is important to teach your pet that staring from humans is fine.

Have you ever thought about what effect the way you physically communicate with your dog has on his mental and physical well-being? While you imagine that a good-natured thump or strong patting on your dog's rib or back, or even a boisterous 'wrestle' or ear-fondling session, signifies your affection for him, such treatment is likely to be uncomfortable or even downright painful for your pet. Try it on yourself and you'll see what I mean. Gentle stroking is the best way of indicating your love and regard for him.

Vocal communication

A dog's hearing is much more acute than ours. Loud noise, therefore, causes dogs discomfort and fear. Don't raise your voice in anger towards your dog, subject him to blaring music or loud volume from the television. In addition, avoid sudden movements or loud noises directed at your dog, which he could construe as being aggressive. Dogs respond best to gentle, low and soothing tones – they may not understand the words, but they do understand the meaning conveyed through the tone of voice. This applies equally when you use harsh tones.

Playing correctly with your puppy will help you form a strong bond with him.

PICKING UP YOUR DOG

1 Crouch down and gently but firmly gather your dog to you, with one arm around his chest to keep him from breaking free and the other arm under his bottom for support.

2 While keeping the dog close to your body, so that he feels safe and secure and can't jump from your arms, stand up slowly.

3 Carry the dog close to your chest. To put him down, simply reverse the actions. Throughout, bend from the knees to avoid straining your back.

See page 118 for how to handle and move an injured dog.

Compared with children, dogs are less able to understand sounds used as signals and find it harder to learn vocal commands, such as 'sit' and 'come here'. It is much easier for them to learn such spoken commands if they are given in conjunction with hand signals or gestures during training. The hand signal can be gradually withdrawn as the dog becomes more familiar with the vocal commands.

Give him space

Dogs are quick to sense their owners' emotions, and when all is not well they can be upset. Your dog needs a space to retreat to until he senses that you are in a good mood and ready to give him attention. This 'sanctuary' is also a place where he can hide from children, or other pets in the household, when he has had enough of interaction.

Dogs and children

According to research, children who grow up with pets in the house, and who are taught to treat them with respect and care, are more likely to do better at school and develop into well-balanced and responsible adults. If you are a parent, there can be no better reason to have a dog.

It is important that children – and even adult visitors – know not to take liberties with your dog such as grabbing at his tail or paws in play.

Safety

If there are children in the household, they must be taught to respect the dog, and how to handle and speak to him correctly. It is surprising just how tolerant some dogs and puppies can be with babies and young children, but this is not something you should put to the test. You must teach children not to disturb the dog – especially by grabbing at him or screaming – when he is resting in his bed, or eating his food, or he may bite. It is advisable to steer clear of the more naturally aggressive breeds if you have children, and carefully choose one of the more gentle, equable types.

Never leave young children alone with a dog, no matter how good-natured or trustworthy you think the animal is. Often, quite unintentionally, children can harass a dog unmercifully, until he can take no more and bites to warn them off (as he would an unruly pup in the pack). This is unacceptable in a human environment so, for everyone's sake, avoid any situation when the dog and children are at risk.

Interaction and playing

It is important to keep an eye on children when they are playing with a dog. They can get carried away and not realize when a game is getting out of hand, with the dog becoming overexcited and therefore liable to play roughly.

Make sure that your children teach your puppy or adult dog only good behaviour. Show them what to do if the dog jumps up at them or pulls at their clothes, what to do if he play-bites, and how to tell the dog what they want and how to play acceptable games. Show them how to stroke the dog gently and where your dog appreciates being petted. Get your children to help feed the dog, and show them how to tell him to sit and wait for his meal before they allow him to have it. This is to reinforce their pack status over the dog's, and also so that the dog regards them as being rewarding and a good thing to have around because they supply him with food.

Discreetly supervising all their activities together will prevent either party learning or doing the wrong thing.

Hygiene

Children tend to put their hands in their mouths at every opportunity. Although it is rare for a child to pick up any infection (such as ringworm, tapeworm and toxocariasis) from dogs, you must take great care to ensure that children (and adults, including yourself) always wash their hands after handling a dog (and other animals too) to minimize any risk.

Toxocara canis is the parasitic worm carried by dogs and passed out in their faeces that is the cause of toxocariasis in humans. Worming your dog regularly is good practice to keep the risk of contracting toxocariasis to a minimum.

Most infections are harmless if the person concerned (expectant mothers included) has got sufficient immunity against them.

Playing together is a great way of expending excess energy in both your dog and your children.

Discourage children from playing tug games with your dog, because they may not know when to stop. The dog could become reluctant to relinquish the tug, and become aggressive towards the child.

Puppy care

For that appealing puppy to grow into the perfect pet, you need to put in lots of work. This will not be hard – common sense, inclination and the will to apply certain training principles and procedures into training your puppy how to behave and perform as you wish him to will do the trick nicely.

Handling, interaction and socializing

Establishing yourselves as higher in rank than your puppy is one of the most important and kindest things you and your family can do for him as he grows into adolescence and adulthood. By firmly establishing his place at the bottom of the pack, you are helping to ensure he has a much better quality of life when he grows up than a puppy that has been allowed to run riot and have all his own way.

Usually, an existing adult will accept a puppy without problems, because the puppy does not represent a threat.

See pages 58–59 for how to handle dogs, pages 60–61 for how to integrate dogs and children, and pages 50–53 for information on training and socializing.

Feeding

If you get your puppy from a rescue centre or reputable breeder, ask for a diet sheet detailing the food type, how much of it and how many meals a day he is receiving. Carry on with this, being sure to follow the life-stage feeding guides on page 28 as your puppy matures, to ensure you meet his nutritional needs.

Playing

After eating and sleeping, play comes high in a puppy's priorities; indeed, this is essential for his development. He will amuse himself for ages with an assortment of toys (an old sock knotted in the middle provides a cheap but highly enjoyable plaything) and, of course, his human playmates. Any toys you give him must be suitable for puppies, and you should replace them if they become dangerously damaged, so that the pup does not swallow torn-off pieces that may cause serious digestive disturbances or blockages.

The more games you play with your puppy, the more he will consider you to be the most interesting thing in the world. The more he wants to be with you and please you, the easier he will be to control. Such dogs are much more fun to have around.

BIRTH TO REHOMING

For information on caring for puppies from birth to rehoming, see pages 112–113.

Praise and reward

Dogs love being praised and rewarded, and normally learn very quickly which types of behaviour reap good things; they will therefore strive to attain these from you. Learning which acts gain praise and reward, and noting those that don't is a vital part of a dog's education – and it also forms the basis of the quickest and most pleasant way to train him.

Discipline

Only rarely should you need to correct your puppy. Most of your interactions should be happy and pleasant, which will mean you become a good friend and your puppy will try hard to please you. Manipulate situations so that he does the right thing and can be rewarded for doing so, rather than allowing him to do something you don't like and then telling him off for it.

If discipline is necessary, give it in a similar way to how a bitch would discipline her pups. It should be immediate, startling, non-violent and over in seconds. Then show him the correct behaviour and reward him for doing it. If he is about to do something unacceptable, warn him not to first. Do this by saying 'No!', 'Arghhh', or something similar, in a deep, stern and growly voice.

If he continues with what he is doing, then follow the warning immediately with a correction – before he carries out the unwanted behaviour, such as chomping on your leg. You can surprise him by shouting, growling or clapping loudly at him, thus preventing the intended behaviour. Tower over and stare at him, until he backs off.

If you don't want your puppy to chew things that belong to you, don't encourage him to play with such items or he will, naturally, view them as fair game.

You may have to push him away at the same time if he persists. Then show him that the correct way to behave is more rewarding. For example, if he sits quietly, revert to being calm and pleasant and reward him.

It is important to tailor the level of the correction needed to your puppy – some are more sensitive than others. If, after a correction, your puppy appears sulky and wary of you, you are overcorrecting, and if he carries on doing the things you have previously corrected, you are under-correcting.

Handling and grooming

Your puppy needs to learn to be groomed, hugged, touched and restrained on your terms. The more puppies are familiarized with these procedures, the less they feel threatened by such experiences and the less likely they are to bite when touched, particularly during stressful situations such as visiting the vet. Touching and stroking the puppy all over, as well as holding, gently

Gradually get your puppy used to being handled by lots of people – this is an important part of his socialization process.

hugging and restraining him, builds a trust and an acceptance that will be projected on to people outside the immediate family.

Start grooming sessions as soon as you get your puppy. Keep them short to begin with, gradually extending the time taken to groom him. See pages 65–67 for more information on grooming, and pages 58–59 for more information on general handling procedures.

Oral hygiene

As soon as you get your puppy, get him used to having his mouth opened and inspected, and also to having his teeth cleaned to help prevent plaque build-up and periodontal disease (see also page 102). To clean his teeth, start by rubbing your finger dipped in dog toothpaste on his gums and teeth. Once

he is used to this, progress to using a dog toothbrush, or finger tooth-glove, and gently brush his gums and teeth. Both the toothbrushes and toothpaste are available from pet stores.

Vaccinations

For many reasons, most people are for vaccinating dogs, while others are against (the frequency of booster jabs being a particular issue). However – from the veterinary point of view and due to a lack of scientific evidence to prove otherwise – the balance is in favour of vaccination because there are some unpleasant and lethal diseases that dogs can fall victim to.

Some insurance companies insist that dogs are vaccinated before they will issue policies; if vaccinations are not kept up to date, the insurers may not pay out in the event of a claim, so check the terms before signing up. See page 105 for further information on vaccination.

Grooming

Grooming is an essential aspect of owning a dog. It will help you bond with him, and check for any unusual lumps and bumps, as well as keeping his coat and skin in good condition.

Why groom?

As well as to improve appearance and to help keep him healthy, there are many other reasons to groom your dog regularly:

- Check for fleas, mites and skin ailments.
- Make him easier to handle.
- Keep shed hair around the house to a minimum.

COAT TYPES

TYPE	EXAMPLES	REQUIREMENTS
Wire-haired	• Airedale • Jack Russell Terrier • Border Terrier	These coats need to be brushed daily, and hand-stripped to maintain their shape and appearance three or four times a year; the latter is best done by a professional groomer.
Double	• Old English Sheepdog • German Shepherd Dog • Cross-breeds • Newfoundland • Rough Collie • Golden Retriever	Daily attention is required for some double coats (dense top and undercoats), such as the Old English Sheepdog (it can take up to an hour to groom properly daily), while others with less dense top coats, such as the German Shepherd Dog, are usually fine with a weekly thorough brushing. Some breeds, such as the Old English Sheepdog, Samoyed and Chow Chow, benefit from professional grooming every two months or so.
Smooth	• Cross-breeds • Rhodesian Ridgeback • Labrador Retriever • Rottweiler • Dobermann	A weekly groom should suffice, but you may have to brush your pet more often than this if he has a dense undercoat, such as in the Labrador Retriever.
Long	• Afghan Hound • Spaniels • Setters • Shih Tzu	Daily grooming is required to remove dead hair and knots. If professionally groomed for the best results, this should be done every six weeks, on top of your daily brushing.
Curly/woolly	• Bichon Frise • Poodles • Bedlington Terrier	Curly coats do not moult, but shed hair within the existing coat. Such breeds need regular grooming every other day to remove dead hair, plus professional clipping every six weeks or so to maintain coat shape and style.

• Remove dead hair and prevent the coat from knotting and matting (felting).
• Make your pet feel good as regards his appearance.
• Ensure he is happy to have all areas of his body attended to.
• Help your pet feel more comfortable, relaxed, pampered, and generally better within himself.

How to groom

The method used very much depends on the coat type, and it is wise to ask the breeder to show you how to maintain your dog's coat if he has a high-maintenance coat type. If claws need clipping and hairy inner ears need attention, then again ask the breeder to show you what to do. Otherwise, leave coat trimming and shaping to the professional groomer, unless you intend to learn how to clip, strip and/or trim your dog's coat yourself.

Maintain the coat by brushing or combing out dead hair on a daily or weekly basis, as required. The tools you use will depend on the coat type and density of undercoat. The steps to follow when grooming are as follows:
• Remove dead undercoat – getting right down to the skin, but taking care not to snag or pull it – and tease out knots.
• Brush or comb through the top coat and remove further loose hair.
• Massage a conditioning (protein) finishing spray into the coat to give it a sheen, and remove more dead hair.
• Wipe the eyes, inner ears and under the tail to freshen your pet up. Never poke down into the ears with cotton buds, as you risk damaging the delicate structure inside.

Grooming your dog correctly

1 To begin grooming, put one hand around your dog's chest and shoulders to steady him, and prevent him jumping off the table, if he is on one.

2 Brush the back of the neck, down the back and the sides first, then between the hind legs and under the tummy – taking care not to snag the genitals and nipples with brush or comb teeth, nor to knock bony protuberances with the brush. When brushing, imagine you are brushing your own hair – your dog will soon tell you if you are being too firm or rough.

3 Brush the legs and head last. Be gentle with the head, talking comfortingly to your pet and praising him if he doesn't make a fuss. If he plays up and you are sure this isn't because you are brushing too hard or causing him discomfort, be firm and insist that he stays put to be groomed until you have finished.

Moulting

Shedding of hair in a seasonal pattern is normal in most breeds, but central heating seems to have interfered with the pattern in many dogs, resulting in them shedding hair all year round. Apart from regular grooming, there is little you can do to prevent such shedding apart from perhaps turning the heating down.

Grooming gear

Depending on your dog's coat type – wire-haired, double, smooth, longhaired or curly-coated – you will need all or some of the following:

- grooming glove
- old towels (or similar)
- silky or velvet cloth or duster
- guillotine-type nail-clippers
- round-edged scissors
- straight scissors
- tweezers
- cotton wool
- ear, eye and undertail wipes
- dry or wet shampoo
- spray-on conditioner
- wash-in conditioner
- hairclips (for longhaired dogs)
- tearstain remover

- toothbrush and toothpaste for dogs
- trimming comb and blades
- electric clippers and blades
- de-matting tool
- forceps (for ear hair removal)
- bristle brush
- slicker brush (not suitable for thin-coated dogs)
- rubber brush or slicker (ideal for thin-coated dogs)
- rubber bath mat
- non-slip cloth/mat for table
- baby talcum powder/grooming powder
- box to put the grooming gear in
- fine-toothed (flea) comb
- wide-toothed comb
- stripping stone
- stripping knife
- thinning scissors
- anti-static spray
- coat shedder
- friends to help with handling

If you don't feel comfortable grooming your own dog, specialized grooming is available, but can be expensive.

HANDLING PRACTICE

Getting your dog used to having his ears, eyes and mouth handled from the start will make grooming him easier. Routinely check inside his ears, but not poking inside, wipe his eyes with dampened cotton wool or eye wipes, and lift his lips to inspect and touch his teeth (see page 64 for how to clean teeth). Give him lots of praise during the handling when he allows you to inspect these areas without fuss, so that he views you doing so as a rewarding experience.

Dogs and travel

For every owner, there are times when you have to be away from home – for example, when you are on holidays, visiting friends and family, during hospitalization or when on business trips. During such times, you will have to make arrangements for your dog to be looked after. There are several options to choose from depending on the circumstances.

Boarding kennels

Seek recommendations from vets and dog-owning friends. Visit likely establishments first to satisfy yourself your dog will be well cared for. Your dog will need to be vaccinated against relevant diseases, so ensure his injections are up to date well in advance (see page 105). Take the vaccination certificate with you when presenting your pet at kennels as it will need to be checked. Tell the kennels of any special care your dog needs, or if he has any behaviour problems.

Petsitters

If you have a number of pets, employing the services of a petsitter is a good option. Such a person stays in your house, so you have the added advantage of home security as well as your pets being cared for in familiar surroundings. Use a reputable agency that vets its staff carefully, and offers insurance in case of mishaps.

Leave the following information for pet carers before you depart:
• any specific dos and don'ts regarding your pet's care and handling.

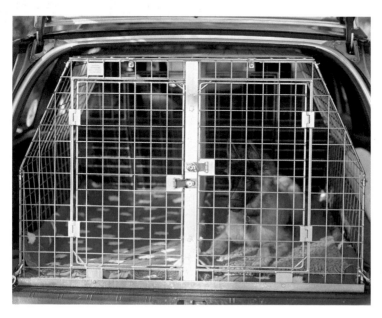

Make sure your car travelling crate allows your dog to lie down, stand up and turn around.

- contact details for yourself and your vet, in case they need to contact you or the vet in an emergency.
- what food your dog has, how much and when; leave enough food for the entire period of your absence.
- any medical details if your dog is receiving treatment.
- maps and duration times of safe, local walks if required.

Taking your dog on holiday with you

If you want to take your dog away with you, you need to accustom him to travelling. If using public transport, check companies' rules and regulations regarding this. In the car, travelling with your dog in a travel crate is the safest option – make sure that he can stand up, lie down and turn around in it. Incorporate plenty of rest and stops in the journey, and never leave your dog unattended in the car – particularly on warm days.

Taking your dog abroad

These days, taking your dog abroad is much easier, thanks to the introduction of the Pet Travel Scheme (PETS). As this scheme is a relatively new ruling, the conditions change fairly frequently, so you need to find out from the relevant government department which vaccinations, ID requirements and parasite treatment are needed for your dog to leave and re-enter your country. Make sure you have the appropriate documentation, that your pet has been vaccinated and parasite-treated within specified times, and that he has the approved ID microchip, to avoid confusion when entering and leaving countries.

Dogs and hotels

Many hotels are pet-friendly these days. Dogs are generally contented to be where their owners are, and are always more than

Check out and book pet-friendly accommodation in the area you intend to visit with your dog well in advance, and ask about any rules and regulations they impose.

happy to explore new places and walks, so both of you are likely to enjoy going away on holiday together. Take your dog's bed, toys, food, collar and leash, and a first-aid kit so you are prepared for any eventuality. When you arrive find out where the nearest vet is in the area. Make sure your dog is wearing an ID tag bearing your holiday address and phone number as well as your permanent one, in case he gets lost while away. Having him ID microchipped is a good idea.

TRAINING YOUR DOG

Although dogs should not be attributed with having human behavioural characteristics, they are intelligent enough to be able to grasp the concept of, and execute, certain actions that their owners require of them – if these actions are requested in a way that dogs find rewarding. So, with this principle in mind, owners have to be clever too, and find a way of training their dog that works quickly and effectively. This section explains how to achieve this ideal – how to speak 'dog' and communicate effectively with your four-legged friend.

The right start

In only a short time, you will be amazed at how much you can achieve in training your dog to respond to your directions and behave as you wish, providing you address it correctly. Don't aim to do everything at once, especially if there is more than one area or problem to deal with.

Commands and rewards

Successful training is based upon a simple principle – reward and withholding reward. Generally, dogs love to please their owners, and enjoy doing so even more when they are rewarded for it. Reward-based training is, therefore, the key to attaining a happy and obedient dog. Rewarding every desired behaviour for a particular word combined with an action will evoke a learned response. Eventually, that response will become automatic every time you say the command or display the action (just like you would automatically check your wristwatch if someone asked you the time).

Food is an all-important aspect of canine life, and therefore food rewards are likely to get the desired behaviour results you require. Food-training (i.e. teaching your dog to sit, stay and wait before he is given his food, and to leave it until he is given permission to eat) marks a good start to achieving obedience in all other areas of behaviour.

Using 'train brain'

• Be consistent in your commands and actions. Stick to the same words for commands, such as 'down', 'sit' and 'stay' as changing words will confuse your dog. Stick with them, even if they take time to sink in. Make sure that all family members use those commands and actions and follow your instigated code of behaviour.

Keep some desirable toys, such as tugs, squeakies, activity toys and bouncy balls, aside (so that they have increased value to the dog) for special rewards when training.

- Reward desired behaviour with food, a favourite toy or attention, and your dog will learn fast.
- Vocal commands should be encouraging and kept at an even pitch.
- Keep commands clear and well spaced out – certainly at first – so as not to confuse your dog.
- If your dog has learnt to ignore a command, and thinks it means something else – such as when you say 'heel' and he is walking ahead of you and pulling, therefore he associates 'heel' with pulling – then change it for another word when you begin retraining (in this case, you could use 'side').
- Never raise your voice or use violence in anger – this is counterproductive.
- Make sure everyone who comes in contact with the dog follows your rules for him. If you don't allow him on the furniture, no one else should either; otherwise you will end up with a bewildered pet.

How long should training sessions last?

Doing too much in one session will overtax a dog both mentally and physically, and he will end up thoroughly confused. Aim to do one exercise – interspersed with play sessions for light relief – until you have perfected it; then move on to the next task. Keep daily training sessions short and fun: 10–15 minutes of concentrated training per hour is the maximum most dogs can cope with. Puppies do not have a prolonged attention span. Three 10-minute training sessions a day are better than one 30-minute session. Always finish on a good note, so that both you and your dog will justifiably feel pleased with, and good about, yourselves.

Keep a diary, so that you can see how progress is going, and note down areas of particular achievement or difficulty, so that

DIY TRAINING TREATS

Most dogs will do anything for a tasty treat. Identify which treats your pet loves and you are on to a winner. Some dogs adore fresh fruit and vegetables, such as dessert apples, tender young carrots and greens, while all dogs are usually partial to sliced hot dog sausage and cooked liver pieces. Some commerically produced treats are also very popular.

you can work on those exercises that your dog finds trickier than others. Above all, stay calm, be patient and make training fun.

All dogs are different

Some dogs learn things faster than others. Large breeds tend to mature more slowly, so you sometimes need to be extra patient with them. Small dogs, on the other hand, can be too clever for their own good and you will have to be on your toes. Bear in mind that working breeds, while intelligent, have an inbred instinct to chase and retrieve, guard or herd, or all three, and require disciplined handling and training to get the very best from them. Such dogs tend to thrive on agility training and training 'tasks', such as retrieving items for you or scent-tracking items. Making training a 'game' is the key to success in all cases.

How long does it take to train a dog?

There are no set time limits to how long it should take to fully train a dog. In fact, setting time limits can be counter-productive if the owner thinks his dog is not progressing as it should. The time it takes to achieve success depends on the aptitude of both owner and dog. Continual training and reinforcement of lessons are what are most effective. This means, for example, that once you have taught your dog to, say, sit, then repeat the lesson often and reward him appropriately so that he does not forget how to respond correctly to commands and directions. Reinforcing lessons learnt on a daily basis help to keep you and your dog 'sharp', and ensures that your dog remains well mannered.

Reinforcement and consistency help prevent bad habits forming. For example, if you allow your dog to push past you when you open a door, he will think it is all right for him to do so the next time – and the next. Similarly, if you let your dog jump around excitedly whenever he sees you get his leash out ready for 'walkies', then he will think that this is acceptable behaviour.

Finding a good trainer will be invaluable in helping you to turn your dog into a well-mannered and controllable companion. A regular training session will help point you in the right direction, as well as be a whole lot of fun. Additional on-the-spot help and advice can't be beaten when it comes to putting into practice what you have learnt on paper. Many trainers will also give you and your dog the chance to try your paws at various activities such as agility, flyball, scenting work and the increasingly popular heelwork to music.

DIY TRAINING TREATS

These meaty little nibbles are the perfect training treats – your dog'll do anything for one.

375 g (12 oz) ox or lambs' liver
1.5 litres (2¹/₂ pints) cold water

1 Preheat the oven to 140°C (275°F), gas mark 1. Grease a baking pan or use a nonstick one.

2 Put the liver in a saucepan with the water, bring to the boil and simmer until cooked through (about 30 minutes).

3 Drain the water into a plastic jug and save it in the refrigerator to add to regular mixer feeds.

4 Allow the liver to cool, then cut it into 1 cm (¹/₂ in) pieces. Place the pieces in the baking pan and cook in the bottom of the oven for 1 hour.

5 Allow to cool, then serve as required. Store in the refrigerator and use within three days.

FREQUENTLY ASKED QUESTION

Q What equipment do I need for training a dog?

A Buying suitable equipment from the start helps make the job of training your dog easier. You would be surprised at what a difference it makes having the correct length of leash for your particular size of dog.

Choose a 'kind' collar such as a half-check (shown above) or a broad collar in leather or nylon, with the weight and width appropriate for the size of the adult dog or puppy. When fitted, you should be able to get two or three fingers under it: too loose and it may slip off; too tight and it will cause discomfort – especially when your pet is eating or drinking. Avoid using a metal 'choke chain' as it can seriously damage the trachea.

Leash type is important. First, it must be comfortable for you to hold; second, it must be of suitable length to maintain a slack tension (see right). If the leash is too short your pet will be dragged along, and if it is too long you will have metres of leash to cope with. Choose a nylon leash that can be extended or shortened as desired, and then you have the best of both worlds.

Puppy Training

A responsible and caring owner will want to guide and train their new puppy into maturing into a well-mannered adult that they can be proud of, and one that everyone will admire, love and want to own. Correctly handling and training a dog from puppyhood helps avoid behaviour problems.

Collar and leash-training

Initially, put a collar on the puppy for short periods of time, with much praise as you do so, then distract him with a game or treat so he gets used to the feel of something around his neck and associates it with a pleasant experience. Once he is quite unconcerned by it, clip on a short lead and allow the puppy to follow you around the house, again for short periods, so he gets used to this extra attachment. Again praise and reward him fulsomely.

Once he is completely happy with his collar and lead on, you can start to teach him to walk by your side while you are holding the lead. Initially when lead-training, keep a reward (toy or treat) in your left hand so that if the puppy becomes distracted, starts pulling or lags behind, you can entice him back to the correct position and pace and then reward him.

Play-training

Where any play interaction is concerned, try to channel games into what will become recall and retrieve exercises at a later stage. If the puppy brings a toy to you and drops it or gives it to you, reward this behaviour. If

An easy way to leash-train is to hold the lead in your right hand and a reward in your left (a tasty and smelly treat or a favourite toy).

Help the puppy learn that the crate is a nice place to be by giving him an activity toy filled with treats to keep him occupied in there.

he relieves himself outside, praise and reward him. If he lies down beside you without pestering for attention, reward him. Use toys to gain his attention – he wants the toy, but will have to work for it.

Puppy-training classes

The best way to socialize your puppy is to take him to puppy-training classes held in a secure area, where he will be introduced to other puppies of his own age and size, as well as to other people. Allowed to intermingle together the puppies will quickly find an acceptable level of chase and play. A good trainer will ensure that play-fighting doesn't get out of hand, and that no bullying takes place and no puppy is made to feel intimidated.

Crate-training

Training your puppy to use a crate happily will come in very handy (see page 22). However, it is important to introduce your puppy correctly to a crate, otherwise it could be viewed as a prison rather than a pleasant and safe place to be. To start with, use toys and treats to encourage your puppy to go inside it, leaving the door open

so he can go in as and when he wants. Put the crate in a quiet, but not isolated, area of the house, so the puppy won't be disturbed while he is in there, but at the same time won't feel abandoned.

Take care not to place it in direct sunlight, or in an area that will get either too hot or cold.

Introducing the crate

• Putting comfy, familiar bedding and his favourite toys in the crate will encourage a pup to go in it and feel at home. The best time to do this initially is after a play session when he is ready for a rest.

• Accustom the pup to going in and staying in the crate by feeding him in there, at first with the door open so he doesn't feel trapped. Once he is used to this, and willingly goes in at mealtimes, feed with the door closed for short periods, and gradually extend these. Remember, though, that puppies generally need to relieve themselves after they have eaten.

• Gradually increase the period of time for which the puppy is left in the crate while you are at home, from a few minutes up to half an hour.

• A crate can be a great tool for toilet-training, but remember that you should only leave the puppy in it after he has eaten and then been outside. Otherwise he may need to urinate or defecate in the crate. Since dogs dislike soiling in or near their beds, having to relieve himself in the crate could make your puppy unwilling to stay inside it.

Toilet-training

Puppies need to be taught appropriate toilet habits; they don't do this naturally. You must expect a few accidents initially, so keep him in an area where it doesn't matter if he deposits the occasional pile or puddle. Be prepared at first to take your puppy for lots of outside visits at the appropriate times, usually after eating, after playing and when he wakes up.

• Define a designated area in the garden with a length of rope. Leaving his last dropping there will indicate to him by sight and smell that this is the right place to go.

• Take your puppy there at the appropriate times and wait until he relieves himself. When he does relieve himself, praise and reward him.

When the puppy relieves himself outside, praise him so he knows that his actions, particularly if in a designated place, were desirable.

Food-training

You need to teach your puppy that it is not necessary to fight for food and that a human near his food bowl does not constitute a threat to his meal. You must also assert yourself as pack leader so the puppy eats only how and when you dictate.

• Have your puppy on a leash and put down his food bowl. Do not allow him to eat, using the leash to restrain him as necessary, along with the command 'leave'. Encourage your puppy to remain quietly by your side, using the command 'stay' with this action.

• Wait until your puppy looks at you for permission to eat, although this may take a while. Eventually he will look to you to see whether you are ready to let him eat. When he does, say 'eat' and allow him to do so. Praise him for his patience.

• Repeat this procedure at every mealtime until your puppy will wait off-leash until he is told to eat. This training method will also enable you to teach the puppy to leave things alone and to stay and wait where you want him.

Attention-seeking and play-biting

Unchecked, jumping up and play-biting often become more and more severe, until the dog is of a size and age where both actions really hurt and frighten human 'targets', especially children. Your puppy must be taught that both habits are unacceptable. To cure play-biting, spray a non-toxic, bitter-tasting liquid (which can be bought from pet stores) on to the area of your body that the pup normally tries to bite (usually the hands and arms). Hold out your hand and let the puppy mouth it. He will usually recoil in disgust at the foul taste and, after a number of repetitions, learn that biting humans is unpleasant. Also follow these rules.

• Make sure members of the family don't encourage the puppy to play-bite. Instead, give him toys that he can chew and play with without harming anyone.

• Handle your puppy's mouth from day one, so that he becomes accustomed to hands being in and around his jaws without biting. Praise him for letting you do this, so he learns that he is rewarded for not biting.

Don't tap the puppy's nose when he bites, as this will merely encourage him to do it even more.

• Don't respond to your puppy when he jumps up. Ignore him, keep your arms folded and avoid eye contact. When he gets down and makes no further attempt to jump up, reward him. This teaches the puppy that jumping up is a negative experience, whereas not doing so is a positive one.

• Most people, especially children, love to say hello to puppies (and to adult dogs) when out walking, but it is important that you ask them to refrain from doing so until the puppy sits and waits quietly for attention.

• Remember to give your puppy attention only when you have first called him to you. When you have finished fussing him, say 'enough' and gently push him away, fold your arms, avoid any eye contact and then ignore him.

• Make sure house visitors know and follow your rules on giving the puppy attention and what to do if he attempts to jump up at them.

If encouraged or left unchecked, play-biting, as a dog grows, can really hurt. You should teach your puppy that biting is unacceptable.

Training juvenile and adult dogs

The key to owning a well-trained dog is to start off on the right track when he is a puppy (see pages 76–79). If you have an adult dog, however, who has not been trained or whose manners leave something to be desired, then he needs to be taught the basic areas of obedience. This section explains how you can train your adult dog in the basics of good manners, from walking to heel on the leash to sitting, staying and behaving well in the house. Some people take these things for granted, expecting a dog to know what is required of him, but that isn't the case. He has to get to know your way of doing things, while you have to get to know him and what makes him tick.

Leash manners

These are important: walking a dog should be a pleasurable experience, not one you dread because the dog pulls you along eager to investigate, or because he dawdles sniffing every post or tuft of grass along the way, full of curiosity.

At first use the word 'heel' only when your dog is in the required position so he learns the word by association. Reinforce the command with a treat or praise so he learns this position is a pleasant one. Once he has learned where 'heel' is you can use the command to return him to that position.

Teaching your dog leash manners

1 *Begin with the dog on your left side, with his shoulder against your left leg and the leash held in your right hand, as shown. Say your dog's name to get his attention, then 'heel'.*

2 *If your dog walks in front of you or pulls, stop. He will no doubt look back in surprise.*

3 *Get your dog back into position and get his attention again as in step 1. Begin walking again. Patiently repeat as required, and your pet will soon get the idea.*

Recall

Once your dog knows his name, you need to train him to come back to you (recall) the instant you call him. This is essential for safety when he is off-leash and running free. If the dog knows that coming back to you means he will be rewarded, he is more likely to comply. Initially, the reward should be of high value, such as a really tasty treat or a prized toy. As your dog becomes conditioned to return to you on command, praise will probably be sufficient, but you can give occasional high-value rewards to maintain immediate response.

When your dog is obediently coming back to you the first time you call him, try the recall exercise in a group of one or two quiet dogs you both know. Approach the other (leashed) dogs with your dog on an extended, long leash. Before they meet and greet, call him back to you. If he responds, reward him lavishly; if not, simply reel him in, drop to one knee as he approaches, reward him as he reaches you and then try again. Once your dog is recalling well in this situation, try him off-leash, but use the leash if necessary. Eventually try the exercise with all the dogs off-leash.

How to train your dog to come back

1 To begin recall training, walk forward with your dog on a long leash and at heel as usual. Then allow the leash to go slack and move backwards, calling your dog's name and the command 'come' at the same time. Offer a treat or high-value toy to elicit a quick response.

2 As the dog reaches you, say 'sit', and when he responds give the treat or play a game with a toy and praise him lavishly. Once he is responding instantly each time you do this exercise, try dropping the leash on the ground (within easy reach) to see what his reaction is. When you are happy that he will come to you immediately on command, try the exercise off-leash in a secure area, gradually increasing the distance between you and your dog.

Sit

Four principles apply to training your dog in the sit position, and these may also be applied to heel-training – the acronym ACER will help you remember them: attention, command, execute and reward.

Be patient when teaching the sit: dogs feel vulnerable in this position and, depending on your dog's history, he may not be very comfortable with it.

If you wish to use treat training to teach your dog to sit, then follow these instructions. Stand beside your dog with a treat in the hand closest to him. Offer the treat, then give the command 'sit' and at the same time move the treat up towards the dog's nose and over his head. Move the treat back past his head slightly so your dog is looking up; he will automatically move into the sit position. As he does, reward him with a treat.

Stay

The ability to get your dog to stay where you want him, both indoors and out, is very useful. For instance, you can use this command if you have visitors and you want your dog to remain in his bed out of the way, or if he needs to stay put for his own safety and that of others while on a walk.

The free stay

Once you are happy with your dog staying on the leash, you can progress to teaching him the free stay. To do this, move away from your dog, command 'stay' and drop the leash on the floor (put your foot on the leash if you are worried about him running off). Wait for a few seconds, then walk to and around your dog, finishing by his right side. Reward him with a pat or a treat – don't hold the treat so that he tries to jump up to get it.

Learning to sit when on a leash

1 *Command 'sit' and simultaneously apply gentle pressure with your left hand on the dog's rear end to push him down.*

2 *Responding to the pressure, the dog will execute the command by sitting.*

3 *When he does so, reward him with the treat. Always request that your dog sits before feeding him or putting him on his leash. This will reinforce good manners, and also your 'number one' status.*

Learning to stay when on a leash

1 To teach stay, have the dog on a leash and put him into the sit position by your left heel.

2 To start, you are simply going to walk around the dog with him in a controlled stay, so command 'stay', with the leash slack in your left hand. Hold your right hand with the palm open in front of the dog as a visual signal. Repeat the 'stay' command and then take one step to his side.

3 Repeat the command, then walk briskly around the dog, staying close to him so he knows where you are. Complete the circuit by standing at your dog's right side. Reward him with calm praise.

4 Repeat the exercise, this time moving a little further away at the front but coming close again at the back to reassure the dog you are still there. If he stays in position, you can gradually increase the distance between you.

Lying down

Once your dog has learned to sit and stay (see pages 82–83), the next step, before progressing to rolling over on to his side, is to teach him to lie down on command.

Instant reward is essential when teaching down, because a dog is at his most defenceless in a lying position. A reward will take his mind off that feeling and teach him that lying on command is both pleasant and non-threatening. Be patient: if you get annoyed your dog will sense it, and you are unlikely to achieve your goal.

USING FOOD TREATS WISELY

A key element that forms the base for all training is food control; follow the procedure on page 78 as the method used to food-train puppies is exactly the same for adult dogs. However, dogs should not be rewarded with food treats forever, or they will become fat. Use treats as part of the daily food ration, not in addition to it. Once your dog understands what you want, give food rewards only intermittently. At other times, give lavish verbal and physical praise, which your dog will appreciate just as much.

Lying down on command

1 With your dog in the sit position, get him to focus his attention on a treat in your hand.

2 Put the treat under his nose, then slowly move it down to the floor or between his front paws. He will sink to the floor in his effort to get the treat. As soon as he does, say 'down' and reward him with the treat and praise. Practise this a couple of times and you will find that your dog soon learns to lie down on command in anticipation of a reward.

3 If all goes well, try extending the lie down into a stay. As you step away from the lying dog, say 'stay' (with a hand signal as shown, if necessary), wait a couple of seconds, then go back to him and reward him lavishly. Gradually extend the distance between you and your dog as you command the stay. You will be surprised at how quickly he learns.

Roll over

With your dog in the down position, you can move on to the roll over exercise. Because exposing his tummy makes him feel vulnerable (to potential attackers), your dog will lie on his side or back only if he feels safe.

Teaching the roll over

1 Show your dog a treat.

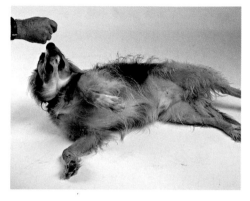

2 Move the treat closer to his nose, then move it slowly around towards his shoulder, over the back of his neck and then down.

3 The dog's head will follow your hand until he has to lie flat on his side to keep the treat in sight.

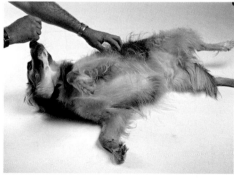

4 At this point say 'roll over', and give your dog the treat and stroke his tummy. Practise until he learns that 'roll over' is a rewarding command to follow.

Retrieve

Throwing a toy for your dog to retrieve is a good way to see that he gets adequate exercise, and it comprises a game that you will both enjoy. If a dog won't retrieve for you, how do you get him interested in playing 'fetch' in the first place?

If your dog won't let go of the toy, don't get into a tug-of-war situation. To make him release it, put him on the leash and command him to sit. Take hold of the toy, but do not pull it; place the thumb and forefinger of your free hand under the dog's muzzle. Apply gentle pressure to his jowls,

pushing them up and over his bottom teeth. At the same time give the command 'give'. The dog will then release his grip and you will be able to take the toy. The intention, of course, is not to hurt the dog, but just to make him a bit uncomfortable until he releases the toy. After repeating this exercise a few times, you will find that as soon as you put your finger and thumb under his jaw, your dog will respond to the command 'give' and allow you to take the toy without a fuss. In future, you will simply be able to call the dog into the sit position, reach for the toy, say 'give' and he will release it.

Retrieve then release

1 Use an everyday (low-value) toy as the item to be retrieved, but have a high-value toy (one that your dog desires above all others) in your pocket, or hidden behind your back to use as the reward once your dog brings the other toy back to you. Have the dog at heel in a sit-stay position (see pages 82–83), then throw the low-value toy, saying 'fetch' at the same time.

2 Once the dog has the toy, call him back to you by saying his name and 'fetch'.

3 Praise the dog lavishly when he returns with the low-value toy, then play a game with the high-value toy. Your dog will soon get the message: no low-value toy, no game. Repeat once or twice, and finish on a win to keep your dog's retrieve motivation high.

Road safety

Knowing how to cross a road correctly with your dog is vital for everyone's safety. He should cross with you, not be dragged across by you, or you by him. There is obvious danger in an owner struggling across a road with a dog that is out of control. In order to be able to cross a road safely, your dog must obey the 'heel' and 'sit' commands (see pages 80 and 82). Only when your dog is sitting calmly and quietly by your side can you concentrate fully on the traffic to make sure the road is absolutely clear before you cross.

Learning road safety

1 *If your dog is not used to traffic, accustom him to the sights and sounds by taking him to a spot where you can safely sit and watch traffic go by. Distract him by offering small pieces of food or a desirable toy. Do not fuss over him too much or cling on to him as you will make him feel there is something to be afraid of. Speak to him in a normal tone.*

2 *Once your dog appears to be unbothered by traffic, walk him quietly along the pavement, again distracting him as vehicles approach. Reward him once they have passed. Soon he will look to you for a reward and take no notice of the moving traffic.*

3 *When crossing the road, stop at a point where you have a good view in both directions. Avoid crossing at corners and junctions, unless there is a pedestrian crossing. Command your dog to sit at the heel position while you check out whether the road is safe to cross. Continue to remind the dog to stay, keeping his attention on you with a treat, toy or verbal encouragement until you cross.*

4 *Cross only when the road is clear in both directions. Keep checking for approaching vehicles and keep your dog's attention on you by having a treat in the hand closest to him.*

A dog who is willing to play is a happy dog. Taking your dog to classes where he can socialize with others will bring out the best in him.

Social skills

A dog who is well socialized with humans and other animals is less likely to develop behaviour problems. The principles of socializing puppies also apply to adult dogs.

If you have an adult dog who has not been socialized properly, you need to address this situation carefully and correctly. The best way to do this is to find a training school that holds socialization classes for older dogs in a safe and controlled environment. Doing this will make you feel more confident, too, especially if you have a dog who gets overexcited or even becomes aggressive when he meets people or other dogs, and you are not sure how to cope with the situation.

Having a dog who will sit and stay on command is the key to successful introduction, integration and interaction. If you can control your dog calmly, you stand a better chance of him accepting the situations around him so that interacting with other people and animals is more likely to be a positive experience for both of you.

House manners

It is important that your dog understands his place in the household and knowing this behaves appropriately. For example, you should be able to greet visitors at the door without your dog rushing to get there first or refusing to let them in.

There are a number of things that you can do to implement house rules that your dog understands. When you come home, do what you need to do first, such as taking off your coat and hanging it up or putting the groceries away. Do anything at all except go straight to your dog and give him attention. While he is rushing around in excitement at your return home and demanding attention, ignore him. You don't want to reinforce his notion that he has high status in the household. After a while your dog will get fed up with being ignored and will either find something to do or lie down. At this point, call him to you and give him a few minutes of your attention.

Make sure that the rest of the family, and guests, also adopt this strategy. When family members or guests sit down, they should be asked to ignore the dog. If he tries to get on someone's lap or a chair, gently but firmly push him down without saying anything to him. Even a reprimand would fulfil his desire for attention. After a few minutes, he will go away. Leave him for a further few minutes and then call him to you, using his name and the command 'come'. Give him a bit of attention, then gently push him away with the command 'finish', and remove your hands and arms from his reach.

By introducing these few firm rules, you will soon see a change in your dog's behaviour. He will not always be demanding your attention or be under your feet. When in the house you have the right to sit and read, relax or work; it is simply bad manners for your dog to put himself in your way or refuse to move.

Solving behavioural problems

'Why does my dog misbehave?' is the most common question dog trainers are asked. Most dogs 'misbehave' because they have been forced into misbehaving because humans have failed to train and stimulate them sufficiently. Before embarking on a retraining programme, first get your dog checked out by a vet to establish that there is no physical reason for his misbehaviour.

There is often no quick-fix solution where some behavioural difficulties are concerned, such as aggression and chasing other animals, so you have to be prepared for a prolonged and sustained programme of retraining, as well as enlisting the professional help of a dog trainer.

A common behavioural problem is when you need to go from one room to another, but your dog also gets up and stands or lies in the doorway, blocking your way. Rather than elevating his status by trying to move him or by stepping over him, it is best to pre-empt the behaviour. As you get up from your seat, give your dog a 'stay' command, which tells him what you want him to do. Provided you have taught your dog this command correctly, he will obey.

Climbing on furniture

If you don't want your dog to sit on furniture, set a precedent and don't let him do it in the first place (from puppyhood), otherwise he will think it is his right.

How to stop climbing on furniture

2 If the dog still won't move, gently but firmly remove him, repeating the command 'off'. If he tries to jump back on, sharply command 'no'. If he tries again, again say 'no' and put him out of the room. Let him back in a short time later and tell him to lie down; if he tries to get back on the furniture, put him out of the room again. He will learn that getting on furniture is unrewarding (he is put out of the room and away from you), whereas by not doing so he is allowed to remain in the room with you.

1 If your dog won't get off furniture when commanded to, hook your finger into his collar to take control and say 'off'.

Attention seeking

If your dog demands your attention by jumping up and pawing at your legs while you are doing something else, such as trying to read, you should ignore him.

How to stop attention seeking

1 *When he gets no reaction from you, he will sit down and consider the situation.*

2 *The dog will then lie down quietly while deciding what his next move should be.*

3 *After he lies down it is important to reward this desired behaviour so he will associate non-attention-seeking behaviour with a pleasant experience.*

Chewing

Dogs who chew things they shouldn't can soon wreck a house and its contents, so it's essential to put a stop to this destructive behaviour swiftly.

Have a number of rattle pots (lidded containers half-filled with pebbles or large dry beans) accessible around the house to use when you see your dog chewing inappropriately.

If your dog enjoys chewing particular items, such as shoes, table legs or soft furnishings, buy a non-toxic anti-chew spray (available from pet stores) and treat those items with it. Then encourage your dog to have a nibble. He will find this most unrewarding because of the very unpleasant taste and won't be likely to try it again.

How to stop chewing

1 *Throw a rattle pot so it lands near your pet (obviously don't aim to hit him with it) to interrupt the chewing. As it lands, the dog will stop chewing or jump away in surprise. If you don't feel confident about your aim, or have a very nervous dog, simply shake the pot hard instead to make a loud noise.*

2 *Quickly replace the item that your dog is chewing with a toy or a chew treat that he can nibble on instead. Encourage him to take it and chew it.*

3 *Give the dog an activity toy filled with something tasty to keep him occupied, especially if you are busy, so he doesn't get bored and go looking for something inappropriate to chew for entertainment.*

HEALTH CARE

Many behavioural and medical problems are caused by the attitude of owners towards their dogs. You can avoid them by making sure that you do all you can to understand and work positively with canine behaviour, as well as by providing your dog with a good diet and adequate exercise, and by being aware of early symptoms that all is not well with your pet.

To keep your pet in the peak of condition it helps to know how your pet's body is constructed, how it works, how to recognize when something is wrong and what to do when your dog is ill or injured.

The canine body

Whatever the breed, dogs are carnivorous and athletic. They have four toes and claws on their front and back paws, plus a fifth toe (known as the dewclaw) that serves no useful purpose; dewclaws are absent from the front limbs of certain breeds. Dogs have 42 teeth – 20 in the upper jaw and 22 in the lower jaw.

The skeleton

The skeleton comprises a semi-rigid framework that supports other softer structures. A system of efficient levers to aid movement comprises the bones of the spine, limbs, shoulders and pelvis (working together with muscles and tendons), while the skull, ribcage and pelvis protect the major organs they contain. Bones are joined together to form the skeleton via tendons and ligaments. Four distinct types of bone make up the skeleton – long, short, irregular and flat bones. Each has a particular function.

Long bones

These long bones are cylindrical and have hollow shafts that contain the vital bone marrow in which the manufacture of all blood cells takes place. They form the dog's limbs, comprising the humerus, radius, femur, tibia and fibula.

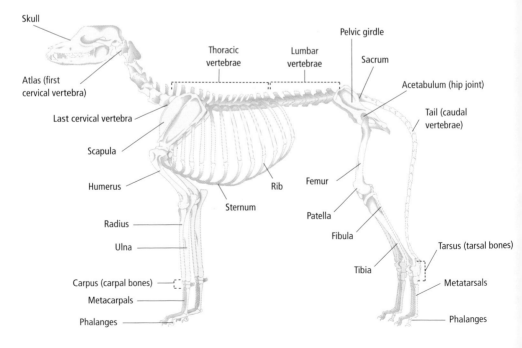

Skull

Atlas (first cervical vertebra)

Last cervical vertebra

Scapula

Humerus

Radius

Ulna

Carpus (carpal bones)

Metacarpals

Phalanges

Thoracic vertebrae

Lumbar vertebrae

Rib

Sternum

Femur

Patella

Fibula

Tibia

Pelvic girdle

Sacrum

Acetabulum (hip joint)

Tail (caudal vertebrae)

Tarsus (tarsal bones)

Metatarsals

Phalanges

Short bones

These short bones consist of a spongy core surrounded by compact bone. They comprise the feet bones and patella (kneecap – where the femur joins the tibia).

Irregular bones

So called because of their irregular shapes, these bones are similar in structure to short bones. A long string of irregular bones make up the spine (vertebral column) and tail. The irregular projections of the spinal column serve as attachment points for the various muscles of the back.

Flat bones

These are made of two layers of compact bone with a spongy layer sandwiched between them, and comprise the skull, pelvis and shoulder blades (scapulae). Flattened and elongated bones make up the dog's 13 pairs of ribs; these bones contain a substantial amount of marrow that produces a proportion of blood cells.

The muscular system

Overlying the skeletal framework is a complex network of muscles that gives the dog its powerful and athletic movement and capacity for endurance as opposed to speed. There are three types of muscle in the canine body:

• **Striped (striated) muscles** (see below) comprise muscle tissue in which the contractile fibres are arranged in parallel bundles, and are attached to the limbs and other parts of the anatomy which are under the voluntary control of the dog, such as movement. These are known as voluntary muscles. Voluntary muscles are usually attached to bones that form a joint. Extensor muscles extend and straighten a limb, while flexor muscles flex and bend the joint. Muscles that move a limb away from the

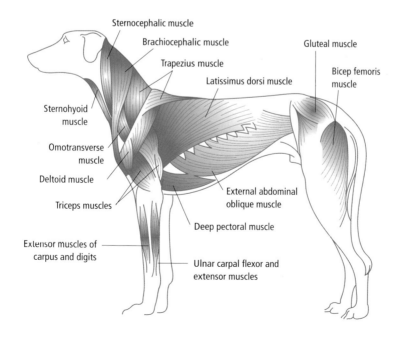

Sternocephalic muscle
Brachiocephalic muscle
Trapezius muscle
Latissimus dorsi muscle
Gluteal muscle
Bicep femoris muscle
Sternohyoid muscle
Omotransverse muscle
Deltoid muscle
Triceps muscles
External abdominal oblique muscle
Deep pectoral muscle
Extensor muscles of carpus and digits
Ulnar carpal flexor and extensor muscles

body are called abductors, and adductor muscles move them back in again.

• **Smooth (unstriated) muscles** carry out muscular functions not under the dog's voluntary control, such as the muscles of the intestines and walls of blood vessels. These are called involuntary muscles.

• **The specialized cardiac muscle** has adapted to carry out the functions of the heart. It possesses unique powers of rhythmic contraction to pump blood around the body via a vast network of blood vessels.

The respiratory system

Respiration provides the dog's body with the oxygen that is vital for life, and expels waste products (in the form of carbon dioxide gas) from the blood. The dog draws in air through his nasal passages via the nose and mouth. This air passes through

LIGAMENTS AND TENDONS

Ligaments are short bands of tough, fibrous connective tissue that connect bones or cartilages, or hold together a joint; they also comprise membranous folds that support organs and keep them in position.

Tendons are flexible but inelastic cords of strong, fibrous tissue attaching muscles to bone.

the throat (pharynx) and down the windpipe (trachea), through the bronchi and into the lungs. Gaseous exchange takes place in the lungs, whereby carbon dioxide from the blood filters into the air sacs, to be exhaled, as oxygen passes from inhaled air to replenish the blood. Breathing is automatic: chest muscles contract, acting like a pump on the ribs and diaphragm, driving air in and out of the lungs.

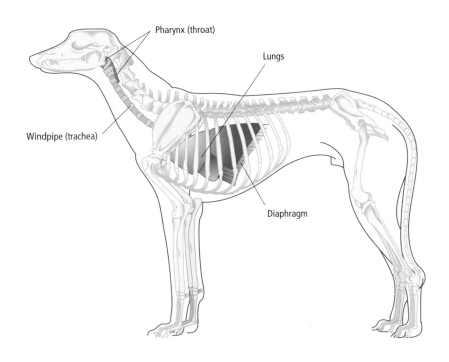

Pharynx (throat)

Lungs

Windpipe (trachea)

Diaphragm

The circulatory system

Every body cell needs a supply of nourishment, and this is delivered via the blood, which also removes waste products from the body. Blood comprises red blood cells and white blood corpuscles that are contained in a fluid called plasma. Plasma contains platelets which contain a blood-clotting agent in the event of cuts and wounds. Red blood cells transport oxygen and nutrients derived from food, while white blood corpuscles collect and transport impurities and bacteria that have invaded the red cells.

Blood is continually pumped around the body via the four-chambered heart, its journey beginning in the left auricle (upper chamber). Oxygen-enriched blood travels from the left auricle into the left ventricle (lower chamber) and on into a great artery (aorta) to run quickly through all the arteries distributing its store of oxygen and nutrients collected from the small intestine. As it releases its 'goodies', the blood also collects waste matter comprising bacteria, dead blood cells and carbon dioxide. The blood then enters veins where, laden with waste products, it begins to slow down on its way back to the lungs to dump its rubbish and be replenished with oxygen and nutrients, before passing on into the heart to repeat its journey.

Red = oxygenated blood (left side of the heart)

Blue = deoxygenated blood (right side of the heart)

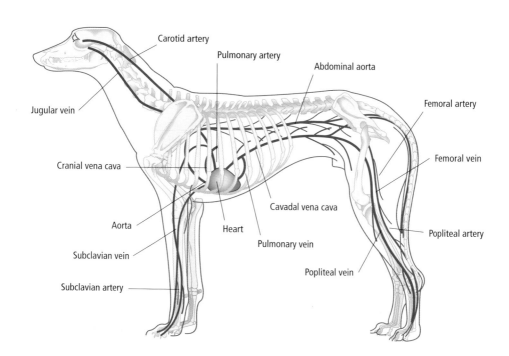

The digestive system

Simply put, the alimentary canal is a type of tube of varying size that runs through the dog from the mouth at one end, to the anal opening at the other. Food enters via the mouth and passes through the tube, where it is digested and all the available nutrients are extracted; what remains is then excreted through the anus.

The tongue laps up fluids and licks up food particles, while the teeth bite at and pick up food to chew it. Swallowing food is aided by saliva, which is produced from three pairs of salivary glands that empty into the mouth. From the mouth food and liquids pass down the oesophagus (gullet) into the stomach. There, acids and enzymes break down the food into chyme (mixture of partly digested food and gastric juices), which then passes through into the small intestine where useful nutrients are absorbed into the bloodstream. The liver aids in the digestive process and neutralizes any toxins.

Once everything of value (fats, sugars, minerals, vitamins, proteins and carbohydrates) has been extracted in the small intestine, the remaining matter passes into the large intestine where excess fluid is removed via the kidneys and bladder to be voided as urine (through the penis in males and the vulva in bitches), before it moves on into the rectum and out of the body through the anus as faeces.

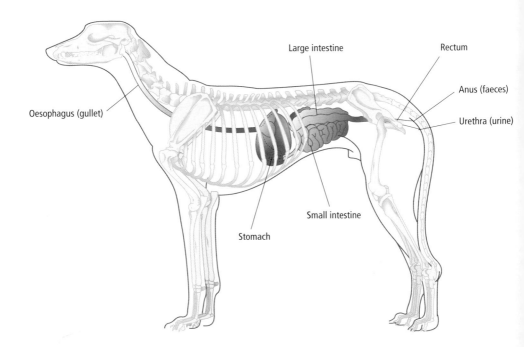

Large intestine

Rectum

Anus (faeces)

Oesophagus (gullet)

Urethra (urine)

Stomach

Small intestine

Skin and fur

The skin serves a number of functions:
- it keeps out foreign bodies
- it keeps in moisture
- it regulates body temperature
- it manufactures vitamin D
- skin pigment and hair protect against ultraviolet radiation
- its glands play an important role in expelling waste products from the body
- it has pain, temperature and pressure receptors.

The three layers of the skin are:
- the epidermis – the outermost layer
- the dermis – the middle layer
- the hypodermis – the innermost layer

Below the hypodermis is a layer of fat that serves as insulation, a back-up nutrient supply and protection for the bones and organs. Unlike us, dogs do not sweat through glands in the skin, except for in the feet.

Canine hair is formed from epidermis and grows through a tube called the hair follicle. Each follicle has a sebaceous gland that secretes an oily, semi-liquid substance (sebum) to lubricate and waterproof the hair and skin. These glands also produce a scent that the dog uses as a marker and chemicals to attract the opposite sex. There are three types of hair:
- **guard hairs** (top coat) are the long waterproof hairs of the top layer of the coat
- **wool hairs** (undercoat) trap air in the coat to help keep the dog warm
- **vibrissae** (whiskers) are hairs that are sensitive to touch, found around the mouth, eyes and on each cheek

Moulting occurs when the dog sheds hair to have a coat suitable for the season. The coat grows and thickens in cold temperatures to help him stay warm.

CHANGES IN SKIN COLOUR

In a fit, healthy dog, the skin is pliable; in a sick or dehydrated dog, it is stiff and unyielding. A sudden change from the normal pale pink colouring can indicate illness and needs veterinary investigation. Any change of colour in the dog's skin is usually first noticed on the lips and gums.
- **White** can indicate anaemia due to parasite infestation, dietary deficiency or even shock
- **Reddening** indicates inflammatory disease of the skin or underlying tissues
- **Blue** indicates heart trouble, respiratory disease or poisoning
- **Yellow** indicates jaundice (liver dysfunction)

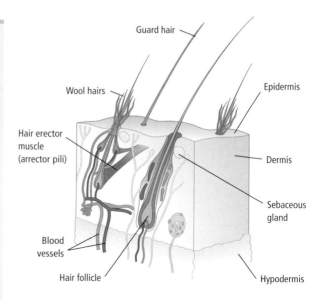

Guard hair

Wool hairs

Epidermis

Hair erector muscle (arrector pili)

Dermis

Sebaceous gland

Blood vessels

Hair follicle

Hypodermis

Canine senses

A dog's nervous and sensory systems are essential to his health and well-being. Perceptions and reactions to his environment are dependent on his senses; movement is controlled through the central nervous system (the brain and spinal cord); and the endocrine system (the hormone-producing glands) controls his patterns of behaviour.

Sight

Canine vision is inferior to human during the day, but is superior at night. Dogs do see colours, but not as distinctly as humans (in pastel as opposed to strong colours), and their peripheral vision is better than ours. In addition to the upper and lower eyelids, there is a third eyelid – the nictitating membrane (haw), which is comprised of a thin sheet of pale tissue tucked away in the corner of the eye. Its function is to help remove dust and dirt from the surface of the eye (cornea) by moving across it during any inward movement, and also to help keep the eyeball moist and lubricated. The eyes are also used to communicate – staring eyes indicate a threat, while 'sad eyes' or looking away indicate submission.

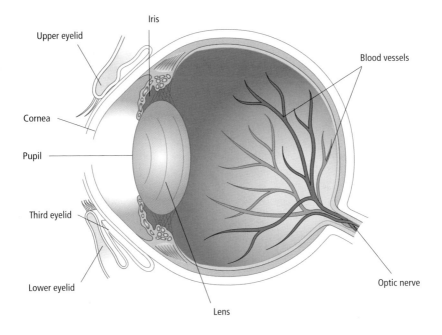

Iris
Upper eyelid
Blood vessels
Cornea
Pupil
Third eyelid
Lower eyelid
Optic nerve
Lens

Hearing

A dog's hearing is vastly superior to that of a human and he is, therefore, more sensitive to sounds than we are – especially those at high frequencies which we cannot hear (hence the use of 'silent' dog whistles). A dog's mobile ears help to pinpoint the source of a sound, since they can be directed towards it. As well as hearing sounds, a dog's ears are also used to communicate via their position to indicate aggression (back), interest (pricked) and submission (down).

Smell

A dog's primary sense is his sense of smell, as it is essential in relation to his sex life and hunting for food and water. The area in a dog's nose for detecting scent is nearly 37 times larger than that in humans, and is approximately 100 times more powerful than a human's. The parts of the brain that process signals coming in from the nose are far greater in size and complexity in a dog than are the corresponding parts of the human brain.

A special organ in the roof of the mouth – the vomeronasal (or Jacobson's) organ – 'tastes' certain smells (such as that exuded by a bitch in season) to help the dog analyse and react to them faster. When the dog is using this organ, he will draw in mouthfuls of air and appear to be 'tasting' it.

When two dogs meet they will usually smell each other's face and then their inguinal regions. Scent plays a significant part in territory. When a male dog marks a prominent object with urine, he is deliberately masking the smell of dogs that have recently passed by, and thereby stamping his claim as 'top dog' in that territory. Faeces are also used as scent markers, with the anal glands discharging a foul-smelling substance unique to that dog.

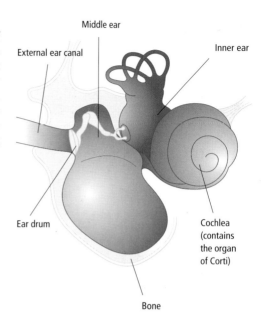

Middle ear

External ear canal

Inner ear

Ear drum

Cochlea (contains the organ of Corti)

Bone

Taste

Whereas humans have taste buds, situated on the tongue, that differentiate between sweet, sour, salty and bitter tastes, the canine sense of taste is thought not to be as well developed – only about one-sixth as sensitive as that of humans.

Touch

Dogs use their noses, mouths and paws to examine objects, after first checking them using their primary sense, smell. The skin is the main touch receptor, and different breeds and types of dogs are more touch-sensitive than others. Dogs that have not been well handled since puppyhood tend to shy away from being touched in sensitive areas, such as the feet, mouth, head, ears, between the hind legs and tails – these are the areas on a dog's body that are vulnerable if attacked.

Routine health care

Keeping an eye on your dog's demeanour, and carrying out simple health checks on a regular basis, will enable you to monitor his state of health.

Daily checks

Some dogs are more stoical than others and will put up with considerable discomfort and pain before their owners realize something is wrong. This is why it is so essential to check your dog over thoroughly every day for any unusual lumps and sore spots. Check his eyes and mouth for foreign bodies or any sign of inflammation, and watch for irregularities in behaviour, eating and excretion. See page 109 for at-a-glance maintenance checks.

Mouth and teeth

Dog breath should not be offensive – tooth decay is easy to diagnose because of the resulting unpleasant smell. The mouth area and tongue should be salmon pink in colour – white gums indicate anaemia, red bleeding gums are an indication of gingivitis and blue/grey gums suggest a circulatory problem. If your dog shows a reluctance to eat or drink, seek veterinary advice.

Nose, ears and eyes

The nose should be clean, slightly damp and free from discharge. The inner ear surface should be clean, smooth

- See pages 106–109 for advice on your dog's body condition, general demeanor, vital signs in eliminations, at-a-glance maintenance checks.
- See page 99 for tips on skin condition.

and odour-free. Smelly or dirty ears need veterinary investigation, as this suggests that infection is present.

The eyes should be clear, bright and free from any discharge. Some brachycephalic (broad-headed) dog breeds often suffer from eye discharge; this is a

Have your vet check your dog's ears if they are smelly or dirty, as these are signs of infection.

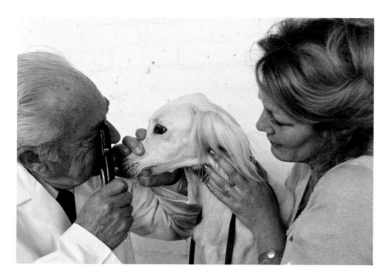

Have your vet inspect your dog's eyes for injury or cataract formation if you notice the surfaces of the eyes are clouding or slightly greying.

result of the skull structure being deformed, meaning that tears cannot drain away as they would normally. Tearstains can be removed with cotton wool dipped in clean, boiled and cooled water, and you can also buy proprietary tearstain removers. Any clouding of the eye surface requires veterinary attention, since this is usually the result of injury or cataract formation. The pupils should be of the same size, and the third eyelid retracted.

If the insides of the ears are looking dirty due to an accumulation of wax, but are not exuding an offensive odour (which requires veterinary treatment), simply gently wipe them with cotton wool moistened with a few drops of olive or liquid paraffin oil.

Ease of movement

Stiffness usually indicates joint problems, and limping suggests a direct pain source, such as a fractured limb, a wound, a thorn stuck in the foot pad, or an infected nail bed. A reluctance to move combined with crying out when you attempt to move the dog may be due to an internal injury or ailment.

Veterinary health checks

Choose a vet who specializes in canine health and cultivate a good relationship with them. An owner who takes their pet for regular health checks and routine vaccinations, and seeks advice on parasite control and dental care, is a valued client for whom a vet will be prepared to have more time. Keeping a diary of your dog's behaviour and health and, therefore, being able to explain any changes you have noticed in detail, is very useful in helping your vet treat your pet appropriately and swiftly when the need arises.

Veterinary surgeries and animal hospitals have reception areas where you can make appointments, pay bills and ask for advice. Many also sell canine equipment and run puppy socialization and regular weight-watching clinics.

If for any reason you feel you would like a second veterinary opinion, then it is within your right to ask for one; no one vet knows all there is to know about their particular field of work. Your vet may even suggest that they consult another expert in order to treat your dog appropriately.

Parasite control

Dogs can suffer from a variety of external and internal parasites, including fleas, mites, lice, fungal infections, ticks and worms – all of which cause ill health. A wide variety of preparations designed to treat these parasites are available to buy from supermarkets and pet stores, but they are not as effective (nor often as easy to apply or administer) as those which are available on prescription from your vet. You must also treat other pets in the house, and the house itself, with treatments (also available from vets), or reinfestation will occur immediately. Vacuum-clean carpets and the place where your dog sleeps regularly, and wash your pet's bedding every week or so to destroy flea eggs.

Intestinal worms (roundworm and tapeworm) are most efficiently controlled

CONTROLLING FLEAS AND TICKS

There are various product options for flea and tick control and prevention available from vets, comprising sprays, which are effective for up to three months, spot-ons (effective for one month, also called drop-ons) and pills (effective for one month). One particular flea product will also kill roundworm.

Fleas bite the dog's skin in order to feed off their blood, with the resulting bites causing intense itching that can lead to severe dermatitis. If your dog scratches himself constantly, check his coat for signs of fleas. Heavy flea infestation can cause anaemia, leading to death if left untreated.

Ticks are blood-sucking parasites that cause itchiness, infection and even paralysis in some countries. Never try to pull a tick off the skin. Its head may be left embedded, which will lead to infection. A dab of surgical spirit (or flea spray that kills ticks) will make them release their grip.

by an all-in-one treatment prescribed by your vet. Deworming products available from vets come in granule, pill, liquid or paste form.

Administering internal medication

Only give medication as prescribed or advised by your vet, and administer any medicines or pills strictly as directed.

If you are given a course of treatment for your dog, then ensure you complete it. If the treatment course is incomplete, then it is not likely to have the desired effect. This is not only a waste of your money, but your dog will continue to suffer unnecessarily. If you have difficulty getting your dog to take his medicine, then ask your veterinary practice staff for advice or help.

Liquids

Using a syringe (your vet can supply this) is often the easiest way to give liquid medicine to your dog. Simply insert the nozzle in the corner of the mouth and squeeze out the contents a little at a time, stroking your dog's throat to encourage him to swallow.

Pills

Some dogs will eat pills straight from your hand, or embedded in a morsel of tasty food. If these cannot be given in food, then follow these steps:
• hold your dog firmly.
• tip back his head.
• open his mouth.
• pop the pill at the back of his throat.
• close his mouth.
• stroke his throat to encourage him to swallow the pill

Applying topical (external) treatments

Only use treatments prescribed or advised by your vet, and apply them strictly as directed. When administering drops or ointment to the eyes, hold the dog's head

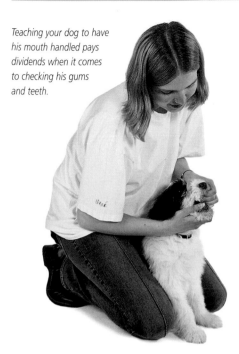

Teaching your dog to have his mouth handled pays dividends when it comes to checking his gums and teeth.

still (or get someone to hold him for you) and aim for the centre of the eye, or wherever directed by your vet.

To apply ear drops, hold the head still, squeeze in the drops as directed, then gently massage the base of the ear to ensure the liquid is evenly distributed on the affected area. When applying ointment to wounds, gently massage it into the affected area with a clean finger. In cases of zoonotic diseases, wear rubber or plastic gloves for each topical application and dispose of them safely in the rubbish bin afterwards.

Vaccinations

Dogs, like every other mammal, are susceptible to certain viral diseases, some of which can prove fatal. While they will not pass these on to humans (apart from rabies), they will transfer them to other dogs, and also cats in the case of the *Bordetella bronchiseptica* (Bb) bacterium

(responsible for kennel cough). It is advisable to have your dog vaccinated for the following reasons:
- to help prevent life-threatening disease.
- to help prevent spread of disease.
- to help eliminate canine viral diseases.
- to enable you to book your dog into a boarding kennels when you go on vacation
- to enable you to travel abroad with your dog if required.
- to enable you to enter your dog into dog shows and agility competitions.

When to vaccinate

Vaccinations are given by injection (except the kennel cough vaccine which is squirted up the nose to protect against Bb bacteria and the para-influenza virus; the latter is also contained in the annual booster injection). Puppies and dogs that have not been vaccinated before need an initial course of vaccinations, comprising two injections 2–4 weeks apart. The second jab cannot be given before 10 weeks of age, but the first can be given as early as 6 weeks. Multiple vaccines are usually given in one injection which protects the dog against:
- canine distemper (D)
- canine adenovirus (CAV-2; hepatitis; H)
- parvovirus (P)
- para-influenza (Pi)
- leptospirosis (*L. canicola* and *L. icterohaemorrhagiae*; L)

Immunity for distemper and hepatitis lasts longer than immunity for the other diseases, so an alternating booster jab programme is usually employed whereby immunity to the DHPPi components are given one year and only the PPi and L components the following year. The rabies jab is given separately – routinely in some countries, but not in others that are rabies-free. However, a rabies vaccination is required when taking your dog abroad.

Routine care

Dogs need help from their owners to lead happy, fulfilled and healthy lives. To maintain your pet's mental and physical health, certain routine procedures must be carried out on a daily, monthly and yearly basis.

Body condition

Pet dogs can suffer from obesity if they do not get enough exercise in relation to the food they receive on a daily basis. Being overweight can seriously affect your dog's health and shorten his life. Ask the breeder or your vet what the ideal weight for your dog is so that you can keep track of any deviation from this, which may indicate a health problem. Refer to pages 24–27 for advice on feeding your dog.

Urine and faeces (eliminations)

Important things to look out for are:
• Signs of discomfort when urinating or defecating.

• Unusual elimination, such as defecating/urinating in the house when normally your dog is clean.
• A constant need to eliminate, often with no satisfactory result.
• Blood in the faeces or urine, or other abnormalities such as very loose or very hard stools.
• Not as many eliminations as normal.
• Worms in the faeces (resembling grains of rice or slim, white threads).

Any deviation in your dogs usual elimination should be closely monitored. If this persists for more than a day, seek veterinary advice. If worms are seen in the faeces, deworm your dog.

Straining to eliminate can indicate that your dog is suffering from a digestive or urinary upset. If it persists for more than a day, seek veterinary advice.

Check a dog's pulse rate by placing two fingers on the femoral artery found underneath the skin at the top of the dog's inner thigh.

General demeanour

If you know your dog well, you will notice any difference in his behaviour and demeanour. If he is normally active and perky, but suddenly appears depressed, then it indicates he is feeling poorly. If other signs that all is not well appear, take him to the vet for a check-up. Make a note of the symptoms, so that you can fully inform the vet, which may help him or her to determine what ails your pet. See pages 102–105 for routine health care.

Training

Maintain the rules about what your pet is and isn't allowed to do on a daily basis, so as not to confuse him. Stick to the same vocal and physical commands. Make sure that other members of the family and visitors also abide by these rules.

Special occasion care

At times when celebrations occur, such as Christmas or New Year, dogs need extra-special care so that they do not become stressed with all the noise and extra people in the house, or ill through eating anything unsuitable. Festive decorations and Christmas trees can prove irresistible to curious and playful canines, so make sure that trees are well secured in their stands, lights are plugged into a circuit breaker, and that baubles are shatterproof.

Dogs love to be part of the party, and it is only right that yours should be included as a member of the family, but when you sense he is becoming overwhelmed by all the goings-on, then put him in a quieter part of the house, perhaps with an activity toy to keep him pleasantly occupied, so he can chill out and rest.

Remember that your dog needs extra special care and attention when extra people are in the house, so that they do not become stressed.

Even though you may be tempted to, don't give your dog foods he does not normally receive, such as cakes, sweets and chocolate, otherwise he may suffer unpleasant and painful tummy upsets – but, of course, you can give him his own present of a new toy and a few treats to open with the rest of the family.

Firework use during celebrations seems to be increasing. Most animals are terrified of fireworks, so if they are going off in the neighbourhood keep your dog safely indoors. Having the TV or radio on can help drown the noise. If you are planning a fireworks party, keep your dog inside, preferably in a room on the other side of the house and only buy 'silent' fireworks. Inform neighbours of a forthcoming fireworks party. An advance warning gives them the chance to take precautions against their pets becoming distressed.

AT-A-GLANCE MAINTENANCE CHECKS

FREQUENCY	WHAT TO DO
Daily	• Clean food and water bowls. • Feed and supply fresh water. • Check eating habits. • Check for abnormalities in eliminations. • Exercise and spend quality time together. • Groom longhaired or thick-coated dogs. • Check collar fit. • Check for signs of injury, illness and unusual lumps and bumps. • Train. • Clear faeces from the garden.
Weekly	• Groom shorthaired dogs. • Check ears for wax or hair build-up. • General check for elderly dogs – vital signs. • Check food stocks for forthcoming week. • Wash and disinfect water and food bowls using a pet bowl cleaner or saline solution, and rinse well. • Check for weight loss or gain. • Training class for puppies and juveniles. • Clean teeth.
Fortnightly	• Worm puppies for roundworm and tapeworm – first at 2 weeks of age, and then every fortnight until they are 12 weeks of age; get the wormer from your vet and ask their advice on the correct dosage for your dog. • Training class to keep you and your dog 'sharp' and to help solve or prevent behaviour/obedience problems.
Monthly	• Treat your dog for fleas – ask your vet which product would be most suitable; and whether it is administered monthly or three-monthly (see page 104 for detailed information on fleas and worms). • General health check, including vital signs.
Every three months	• Worm your dog (aged 12 weeks plus) against roundworm and tapeworm; get the wormer from your vet and seek their advice on the correct dosage.
Every six months	• Veterinary check-up for elderly dogs.
Once a year	• Vaccination boosters (see page 105) and general veterinary check-up.

Neutering

You may decide that you want to breed from your dog, and in this case you will know whether you want to raise puppies or set up a stud. If your dog is to be a pet only, however, it is usually best he or she is neutered.

Why neutering is a good idea

The urge to reproduce is intense in unneutered dogs. When sexually mature, an unneutered dog will tend to wander, if he gets the chance, in search of potential mates, risking getting involved in traffic accidents or being picked up as a stray by a dog warden.

An unneutered bitch will come into season twice a year (some breeds, such as the Basenji, only do so once a year) and must then be kept under tight control to avoid unwanted pregnancies, since she will always be on the lookout during these times to get out and mate.

When to neuter

Neutering (spaying in females and castration in males) should be done when the dog reaches sexual maturity at around 6 months old, or at any time afterwards. Individual vets have their own policy on when to spay bitches: some prefer to let them have one season beforehand and spay at around 9 months in order to limit incidences of urinary incontinence afterwards; and some do not spay if a bitch is in season, preferring to wait until 3 months or so afterwards. This is because the reproductive organs are enlarged with an increased supply of blood during the

SPAYING AND CASTRATION

SPAYING

Before spaying: the female reproductive tract comprises the ovaries, Fallopian tubes and uterus (womb).

After spaying: the ovaries, Fallopian tubes and uterus are removed.

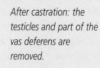

CASTRATION

Before castration: the male reproductive tract comprises 2 testicles in a skin sac (scrotum), connected to the penis via the vas deferens (spermatic cords).

After castration: the testicles and part of the vas deferens are removed.

season and for a while afterwards, so there can be greater risks involved in the surgery.

What's involved

Because the operation is more involved in female dogs, the neutering procedure is more expensive than for males.

Females

The ovaries, Fallopian tubes and uterus are removed under a general anaesthetic. The operation site is shaved and cleaned to help prevent infection, and then a small incision is made mid-line (from the navel towards the hind legs) in order to remove the relevant organs. The wound is closed by means of stitches that are removed about 10–14 days later, unless soluble suture material is used, which gradually dissolves on its own.

Males

The dog is anaesthetized and his testicles (testes) and a small section of the spermatic cords are removed through a small incision in the scrotum; the incision is then stitched as for females.

Pre- and post-op care

The dog must go without food and water for 12 hours before the operation. Most males are back to normal in about 3 days, bitches in 5, and completely themselves again by the time they have their stitches out. When you bring your pet home from the vet's, he will probably still be drowsy from the anaesthetic, so put him in a warm, quiet place to rest undisturbed – with water and a light meal of cooked white fish or chicken – until he feels ready to join in the family activities again. Gently discourage the dog from nibbling or excessively licking the stitches (you may need to put an Elizabethan collar on him if he persists in worrying the wound).

Neuter behaviour

If neutered as early as possible, the behaviour of male and female dogs will be almost the same – at least from the practical point of view of an owner, as both sexes tend to be more affectionate and amenable. There is some truth in the observation that neuters become more inactive than entires as they age (although their life expectancy is greater) as they tend to put on weight, therefore, you may have to adjust your pet's diet and ensure he gets sufficient exercise. Sometimes bitches can become incontinent after they have been spayed, but this can usually be treated successfully with medication. On the plus side, spaying reduces a bitch's chance of developing mammary tumours.

Contraception

Bitches can be given hormone treatment to prevent unwanted pregnancies, but there are drawbacks to prolonged birth-control treatment for there can be serious side-effects such as the development of pyometra (a life-threatening infection of the uterus). Also, it is not 100 per cent effective. If mating has taken place, contraceptive drugs can be used.

Chemical castration (comprising an anti-testosterone drug) is available for males, but again is not totally effective and dogs can, and will, still mate bitches. Side-effects include an increased appetite and a change in hair colour at the site of the injection. Surgical neutering remains the best option to prevent conception.

Neuter policy

Many of the bigger rescue organisations neuter all their animals as a matter of course. Usually, this is because they see, at first hand, the tragedy of too many pets for too few good homes. Neutering ensures that reproduction stops with the dogs that go through their hands.

Reproduction

Species survival depends upon procreation, and pregnancy and birth are the most natural things in the world. A healthy bitch with access to males and a plentiful food supply can produce two litters of puppies a year.

Season

Bitches only mate when they are 'in season' (also known as 'on heat'). They only have one oestrus in each breeding season (usually twice a year and lasting for around 21 days), during which they will accept a mating; this time occurs 10–14 days into the season, once her vaginal discharge turns from bloody to clear.

Looking after the pregnant bitch

Pregnancy in dogs lasts around 9 weeks (63 days). Apart from increasing her diet with food formulated for expectant bitches, treat her as normal. As she becomes larger, she will slow down and become more reluctant to race around. Do not encourage her to run and jump about. If she becomes constipated, substitute one of her daily meals with oily food such as pilchards or sardines.

Prepare a whelping site or box and place it in a quiet area. Line the base with newspaper and cover it with a thick layer of paper towels or washable 'vet bed' fleece. Show the bitch where the 'nest' is, although she may choose her own place.

With longhaired bitches, clip hair surrounding the birth canal and nipples. Sponge her anal area twice a day if she is carrying a large litter and is unable to do this herself. Make sure she is free of fleas and worms before and after birth – consult your vet regarding suitable treatment.

Labour and birth

Once labour starts, the bitch will pace, whining or panting, and look behind her in an agitated and puzzled manner. There will usually be a clear or mucus-like discharge from the vulva and she will lick and clean herself. She will normally refuse food. This stage can last for 24–48 hours.

As second-stage labour begins, the bitch will go to her nest, lie on her side and strain as contractions move the puppies, one by one, down the birth canal. Puppies are normally born around 20–60 minutes apart.

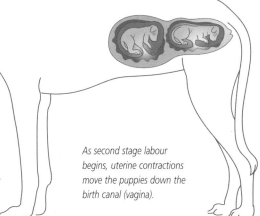

As second stage labour begins, uterine contractions move the puppies down the birth canal (vagina).

After delivering a puppy, the bitch cleans away the membranes, stimulating it to breathe. The placenta is then passed, and the bitch eats it, severing the cord a short way from the puppy's body.

Once all the puppies are born, the bitch will clean herself, then settle down to suckle, curling herself around the pups, and rest. If she goes out to relieve herself, remove soiled bedding and check visually that all the pups seem healthy and content (don't handle them for the first 2–3 days, particularly if it is the bitch's first litter).

Birth problems

If the bitch has been straining for over an hour without results, call the vet immediately so she can be helped.

Sometimes puppies do not survive. If the bitch appears distressed, contact your vet: she may require medication to suppress her milk and help to prevent mastitis. Other problems that can arise during pregnancy or following birth and that need immediate attention from the vet include:
• Miscarriage because of illness or because the foetuses are not healthy
• Uterine infection after birth, indicated by high fever, vomiting, lack of appetite, and dark-coloured, often smelly, vaginal discharge
• Prolapsed uterus indicated by a swollen red mass appearing out of the vulva

Mother care

During whelping, offer the bitch small drinks of water and glucose. After birth, she will probably be hungry and appreciate a light meal of egg and milk, or a meat and cereal broth. She will eat and drink more than normal to maintain her milk supply. Increase her food to around three times her usual amount, split into 3–4 meals a day. Her diet needs to be rich in calcium, protein, vitamins and minerals to sustain her body's needs while lactating, and she needs a constant, plentiful supply of fresh, clean water.

Mastitis

Some bitches may suffer from mastitis due to a bacterial infection. Symptoms of this include hard, hot teats that produce bloodstained or abnormal-looking milk. She will be off colour, and may vomit and have little or no appetite. Call the vet immediately so that she can be treated, and you can be shown how to hand-strip her teats and hand-rear puppies if necessary.

Weaning

At 3–4 weeks, the puppies start to explore outside the nest, and experiment with lapping at liquid foods, and progressing at 4–5 weeks on to more solid nourishment – food formulated for puppies will ensure they receive the nutrients their rapidly growing bodies need. To encourage the puppies to start eating solids, start with a saucer of tepid milk – wipe some around their muzzles with your finger, or gently dip their noses into it, to start them off lapping at it. Sometimes it can take several attempts, but they get there in the end. If they really don't want it, try again the following day. Once they are lapping at the milk, then add cereal to it – leaving it to soften before giving it to the pups. Then progress on to meat-based puppy food. Feed the puppies from shallow bowls so that they can get at the food easily. As they eat increasing amounts of solids, their excreta changes – now it is time to put newspaper down.

Bitches naturally wean their puppies as their milk dries up 5–6 weeks after the birth. At this age, the puppies should be fully weaned on to solid puppy food. By 8 weeks, the puppies are usually fully independent of their mother for food and hygiene, and are ready for homing.

Stages of growth

Newborn

Puppies are totally dependent on their mother and her milk for the first 3 weeks. After this, they begin to experiment with eating the solid food that their dam brings back in the form of prey for them to eat, or that their human carer provides. Keeping her puppies clean is a vital role for the mother, whose babies might otherwise die of disease. The mother continues to wash them all over until the babies learn how to do this themselves; she also prompts them to relieve themselves by licking their genitals.

2–3 weeks

Begin to handle the puppies from 2 weeks old to start the vital canine-human socialization process. At this age, the mother will not be too anxious about familiar humans touching her babies. During this period, the puppy's teeth begin to appear and he will learn to walk and lap liquid puppy food such as milk and porridge. He also develops the ability to urinate and defecate unaided by his mother, and his senses of smell and hearing begin to operate.

4–5 weeks

By now, the mother will begin to discipline her puppies with a growl, usually to prevent them feeding at will. By the age of 4 weeks, puppies can see more clearly and they can stand quite well and toddle around on short, unsteady legs. At this stage they can roll over and right themselves, and play with their siblings and carry objects in their mouths. By the end of the 4th week their senses are more efficient and puppies are curious about their environment. By the end of the 5th week puppies can move around confidently and can often run and balance well.

6 weeks

Facial and ear expressiveness are evident and the puppy has full use of his eyes and ears. Dominance and hierarchy games will be seen among litter mates. Weaning on to puppy foods proper can now be introduced as he will no longer be totally dependent on his mother's milk and, as his milk teeth are as sharp as needles, she will be reducing the amount of time she feeds the pups (see page 28 for feeding guidance). First vaccinations can be done at this age.

7–19 weeks

Second vaccinations can be done at 10 weeks. Puppies are usually by now fully weaned and well socialized with humans, and preferably other animals too, and are ready to go to new homes for their obedience and socialization training to continue. House training should begin, as should name and lead training.

Juvenile (12 weeks to 6 months)

*Puppies are eager to please their owners.
Chewing and mouthing behaviour is common
as the puppy is teething, so he should be given
appropriate toys on which to do so. He should
also learn to inhibit play-biting behaviour with
humans and it should not be encouraged. At
this stage he should learn his place in the human
family, that is at the bottom of the pack,
otherwise he may try to exert dominance over
them. Manners and obedience training should be
done on a regular basis – the older the puppy
gets, the better his concentration and ability to
learn will become.*

Adolescent (6–18 months)

*During this period, the puppy becomes much
more independent and is likely to challenge
authority. Sexual maturity is reached; bitches
come into season, with associated behavioural
changes, and males experience dramatic
fluctuations in male hormone levels. Territorial
behaviour begins to develop. This is the most
difficult time for owners to live through, and
the time when many people give up their dogs
for rehoming. If you have laid down solid
foundations of good behaviour up to this
point, adolescence will be less wearing for
all concerned.*

Adult (18 months and over)

*The dog will now be physically mature, albeit
with some filling out to do. His character is fully
formed although some refinements will still be
occurring. Young adults continue to develop in
character and will finally settle down at about
3 years of age. Refinement and continuation of
training is needed, but if owners have done their
job well, they can relax and enjoy many years
with their well-balanced, sociable and obedient
four-legged friend.*

First aid

Accidents usually happen when least expected, so it is sensible to be prepared at all times. A knowledge of first aid can be useful and, in some instances, essential. Emergency situations need immediate action; if you know what to do, you may be able to limit the injuries sustained by your dog, and perhaps even save his life.

First-aid training

Having a basic training in the subject will give you the confidence to deal with an emergency situation calmly and efficiently until an expert practitioner can take over. Some veterinary clinics run courses in basic first aid.

First-aid basics – ABC

The basic principles of first aid are as simple as ABC – Airway, Breathing, Circulation. The priority is to make sure the dog's airway is clear to enable him to breathe and ensure blood is circulating properly (that his heart is beating). When satisfied, you can deal with any other symptoms as appropriate.

Airway and breathing

If the dog is unconscious in a collapsed state, check that he is breathing. If there is little or no breathing and the tongue is blue-black, open the mouth and remove anything blocking the airway. Gently lift the chin to extend the dog's neck to open the airway. If he still does not breathe, administer artificial respiration:

• Hold the mouth shut and cover the nose with your mouth.
• Gently breathe up the dog's nose – 30 breaths every minute (taking your mouth from his nose between breaths to allow for exhalation).
• With a small dog, an alternative method of artificial respiration is to hold him by his hind legs and, keeping your arms straight, swing him to the left and then to the right. This transfers the weight of the dog's internal organs on and off the diaphragm, causing the lungs to fill and empty of air. **Caution:** never try this if an injury is suspected that may be aggravated by using this method.
• Keep artificial respiration up until the dog begins to breathe on his own, veterinary help arrives or you believe the dog to be beyond help.

Circulation

Next, check for a heartbeat. Do this by putting your ear on the dog's chest on the left side, just behind his elbow, and you will be able to hear it. Also check for a pulse – place fingers in the same position as your ear, or on the inside of the dog's thigh in the groin area. If there is no heartbeat begin chest compression as described below – the techniques vary with the size of the dog.

• For small dogs, squeeze the chest with your hands. To do this, place one hand either side of the dog's chest, just behind his elbows, and squeeze and release the chest in a smooth action, giving two compressions every second. Always use the flat of the hand, never the fingers. Don't use too much force, as it is easy to break the ribs.
• For larger dogs, place both hands on the dog's left-hand side, about level with his

First-aid kit

Basic first-aid items can be bought from your vet, local pharmacy or good pet stores. A first-aid kit should contain the following:

absorbent paper (kitchen) roll
antihistamine to ease insect stings and bites
antiseptic lotion for cleaning wounds
antiseptic wound powder
bandages
conforming ('sticky') bandage
cotton buds
cotton wool
curved, round-ended scissors
dog nail clippers choose the guillotine variety
Elizabethan collar
glucose powder to make rehydrating fluid
heavy-duty protective gloves
kaolin pectate for diarrhoea

KY jelly or vaseline to lubricate a thermometer
muzzle – a basket muzzle is best
non-stick dressings useful for cuts
pencil torch and batteries
rectal or aural thermometer – digital ones are easiest to use
round-ended tweezers
small stainless steel or plastic bowls
space blanket or large sheet of bubble wrap
squares of clean cotton material for wounds
sterile eye wash or contact lens saline solution
sticky surgical plaster tape
styptic pencil to stem bloodflow from minor cuts or bleeding claws; it stings, so muzzle the dog first
surgical gloves
surgical spirit to remove ticks
syringe plunger to administer liquid medicine
table salt to make saline solution

elbow. Apply steady pressure and release the pressure at the rate of two compressions per second.

Whichever method you choose to use, give two breaths to the dog for every four compressions. Keep checking for a heartbeat or pulse throughout your attempts at heart massage.

Moving and lifting an injured dog

Don't move an injured dog unless you have to, as any movement may aggravate his injuries. However, if it is imperative that he is moved, see page 59 for the safe lifting and carrying technique. You may need help to move a large dog safely; if you are alone, you can move a large, unconscious dog by gently and smoothly dragging or rolling him on to a coat or blanket, and carefully dragging him to safety. Muzzle him before you move him.

It is easier to restrain, examine or treat a dog at waist height; so, if possible, place him on a table or bench – cover this with a blanket or other material to prevent him slipping and panicking. Restrain him gently

An injured or ill dog should be covered with a 'space blanket', blanket or towel to keep him warm and help alleviate shock symptoms while waiting for veterinary attention.

but firmly while you assess what should be done next. Placing your hand over his back and under his chest will allow you to hold him firmly and safely while you apply appropriate first aid.

Basic first aid

The most common dog injuries occur when your dog or puppy is going about his normal business. A basic understanding of first aid will be invaluable in treating these.

Burns and scalding

Cool the burnt area with iced water (if you can stand the dog in a bath or sink, pour cold water on the affected area for about 10 minutes) to reduce the pain and the severity of the burn. Then cover the burn lightly with a cool, damp clean cloth (handkerchief or drying-up cloth), wrap the dog in a space blanket and take him to the vet.

Chemical burns

To prevent the dog licking the area, muzzle him. Put rubber gloves on and wash the affected area under cold running water – either by standing the dog in the bath or sink and running water over the burn, or using a hosepipe in the garden. Follow the instructions as for burns and scaldings.

Sunburn

Treat as for burns and scaldings.

Poisoning

If you suspect that your dog has eaten poison (profuse salivating is the most obvious sign, while sleepiness can indicate ingestion of rat poison), contact your veterinary practice immediately and tell them what has happened. This will give them time to get the relevant information from the manufacturer while you get your dog to them.

Only if you are instructed by the vet to make your dog vomit, place a couple of washing soda (sodium carbonate) crystals on the back of the dog's tongue. Alternatively, use mustard or salt mixed with a little water. Get the dog to the veterinary clinic as quickly as possible.

Broken bones

Signs of fractured bones – apart from them protruding from the skin – include extreme pain on moving a limb, swelling, tenderness, loss of control and deformity of the limb, unnatural movement of the limb, or the sensation (or sound) of the two ends of the bone grinding against each other (crepitus). Keep the dog as still, quiet and warm as possible and contact your veterinary clinic to ask what to do in these circumstances.

Supporting the injured limb with bandages and a splint is preferable, but this should only be attempted by an experienced and competent first aider.

Electrocution (electric shock)

Once the power supply has been turned off, check that the dog is breathing – if not, begin artificial respiration (see page 116). If it is not possible to switch off the power supply, don't approach the dog. Electrocution will almost inevitably cause burns, which will need treating as described on page 118.

Insect stings and bites

A dog will usually yelp and paw at the area of his body where he has been stung. If the dog has been stung in the throat, seek veterinary attention immediately.

For stings elsewhere on the body, clip the fur from around the affected area so you can see what the problem is. Wash it with saline solution: bees leave their sting in the victim, wasps do not. If you can see the sting and judge it is removable with tweezers, then do so, and then wipe the area with cotton wool dampened with surgical spirit. Neutralize wasp stings with vinegar and bee stings with bicarbonate of soda. Dry the area thoroughly, without rubbing and apply a wet compress. For other insect bites, clean and dry the area, and apply antihistamine spray or cream.

Bite wounds

Dogs are at risk from three main types of animal bite – dog, rat and snake.

• For dog bites, clip the fur away from around the bite and clean the wound thoroughly with saline solution, followed by diluted antiseptic lotion. Dry the area, and then apply a liberal dusting of antiseptic wound powder. Repeat twice daily.

• Rat bites are especially dangerous, as they carry many harmful diseases. Treat as for dog bites, and then take your pet to a vet who may administer an antibiotic injection and prescribe an antibiotic dusting powder.

A dog is lame if he is incapable of normal locomotion, or moves with an abnormal gait.

• Keep dogs bitten by a snake as calm as possible and prevent them running around, or even moving. Seek immediate veterinary attention.

Drowning

Once the dog has been pulled from the water, hold him upside down (or lift his back end up if a large dog) to drain the water from his lungs. Then lay him flat and rub his body fairly vigorously to promote respiration. If he is not breathing, start artificial respiration (see page 116) and get veterinary help as soon as possible.

Foreign bodies

Most foreign bodies lodged in an area of the body are best left to a vet to remove. If the dog is pawing at the affected area, gently restrain him to prevent further damage occurring until your vet takes over and deals with it. Grass seeds can sometimes be flushed out of the eye using a syringe filled with saline solution, while thorns can often be extracted from paws fairly easily – but check that the end has not broken off and been left in the wound. If this happens, seek veterinary treatment.

Choking

Choking warrants immediate action: take a secure hold of the dog and open his mouth to see if there is anything stuck in his throat. In trying to remove a foreign object, you must not push it further down the throat and make matters worse. If you have a helper, ask them to hold his mouth open while you remove the blockage.

If whatever is blocking the airway is wedged in place, don't try to pull it out; instead, sit down, hold the dog's hind legs, lift them over and hold them between your knees. Place one hand either side of the chest and squeeze using jerky movements, making the dog cough. Squeeze 5–6 times, and the dog should cough out the object.

Let your dog rest, and then take him for a veterinary check-up. If the object does not come out, don't rest your dog, but take him to the vet immediately.

Fits and convulsions

Do not hold down a fitting dog – take away any objects around him that he could harm himself on, and seek veterinary attention urgently. Seizures are potentially life-threatening.

Lameness

If your dog suddenly becomes lame, is unable to bear his weight on one or more of his legs, or cannot walk, check for cuts, foreign objects lodged in a limb or paw and also for broken bones. Keep him still until a vet can examine him.

Shock

Shock comprises an acute fall in blood pressure after an accident, injury, illness or serious fright, and is life-threatening. Signs of shock include: cool skin, pale lips and gums; faint, rapid pulse; staring but unseeing eyes. Keep the dog quiet and warm by wrapping him in a space blanket and promote blood circulation by gently but firmly massaging his body, taking care not to aggravate any injuries in doing so. Seek veterinary attention as soon as possible.

Bleeding wounds

Most cuts and lacerations heal on their own fairly quickly; keep them clean with cotton wool dampened with saline solution. Initial bleeding, which may be profuse, helps clean the wound of debris, lessening the possibility of infection. Seek veterinary attention immediately if:
• the wound is spouting bright red (arterial) blood in jets.
• a constant flow of dark red blood refuses to cease.

PREPARING A WOUND

To clip fur around wounds, use a pair of scissors with curved blades and rounded ends. Dip the blades in clean, preferably boiled and cooled water, and then carefully clip the fur around the wound. The fur will stick to the wet blades, preventing it from fallling into the wound. Dip the scissors into the water again to swill off the fur clippings.

• the wound is deep or serious enough to cause concern, as sutures may be required.
• gunshot wounds are suspected.
• the skin has been punctured – these wounds appear tiny on the surface, but can be quite deep and are, therefore, particularly prone to becoming infected. Never attempt to remove a foreign object from such a wound as this may aggravate the injury and allow large amounts of bleeding to occur.
• cuts affect toes or a limb as tendon damage may have occurred.

For minor wounds, blood flow can be stemmed by gentle direct pressure using a dampened clean pad of cotton material, before cleaning them. Where arterial or venous bleeding is present, apply indirect pressure (not on the wound itself) to the appropriate artery or vein if you can feel it on the heart side of the wound; otherwise press a cotton pad over the wound to help stem the flow of blood. Elevating the injury, if possible, will enable gravity to help reduce the blood flow.

Internal injuries

These can be detected by swelling of the abdomen, bleeding from the mouth, nose, ears, eyes, sex organs or anus; bloodstained urine or stools, shock and signs of bruising on the skin. Seek veterinary attention immediately.

The older (senior) dog

An ageing dog, if he is in good health, can provide companionship that is just as rewarding as playing with a puppy. The old dog's reactions may not be as sharp, nor may he move as fast or be as agile when playing 'fetch' with you, but you and he will gain as much pleasure from your relationship as you did when he was younger. He may sit around a lot and be undemanding and quiet, but an elderly dog should not be ignored.

Signs of ageing

Signs of old age in a dog are not difficult to spot: he starts to take things easy, spends more time than usual sleeping, and his ease of movement lessens; some dogs suffer failing eyesight and hearing. In black-coated individuals, grey areas around the muzzle develop and sometimes close to the eyes, although the overall body colour is unaffected.

With bad or worn teeth or inflamed gums, old canines will find soft, moist or semi-moist foods easier to eat.

Lifestyle

Everything should be done to keep the elderly dog feeling as good as possible. Disturbed behaviour patterns may be the result of chronic physical or mental illness. For example, a previously clean dog may have 'accidents'. If this happens, it may be best to keep your pet in areas of the house where such accidents don't matter – but do not shut him away or limit his access to his family, as this would be unfair and stressful.

If your dog has remained fit and active throughout his life, carry on exercising him as normal on the basis that 'if he doesn't use it, he will lose it'. He will tell you when he needs to slow down, and providing you are alert to your dog's needs you will know when and how much to ease off.

If his eyesight and hearing begin to fail, he can still enjoy life, but you may have to adapt your command signals to him so he can understand what you want. Clapping can help a blind dog, while visual signals can direct a deaf dog.

Diet

Foods specially formulated for senior dogs are available, and these contain all the nutrients the ageing body needs to remain in the best possible condition and help delay or alleviate the onset of conditions such as senility. As older dogs often suffer from liver-failure problems, a low-protein diet may be applicable; consult your vet regarding the best type of food for your dog. Older dogs are often unable to defend their food as they once could, so if you have other dogs make quite sure they are not allowed to steal his meals, perhaps by keeping them in a separate room as he eats.

Common ailments

As a dog ages, so a certain amount of body tissue degeneration occurs. This is inevitable, although with owner and veterinary care the effects can be eased. Once your dog reaches the age of 7 (or 5 if it is a giant breed) you should take him for twice-yearly veterinary check-ups, so any problems can be diagnosed and treated at an early stage. Old dogs are prone to certain ailments that include:

• liver disease
• joint stiffness and arthritis
• coat and skin complaints
• constipation due to decreased digestive efficiency
• tooth and gum problems
• injury due to decrease in agility
• cold-related problems due to decreased body temperature regulation
• incontinence
• senility
• hearing and sight problems
• obesity-related problems
• loss of appetite
• heart disease

Seek veterinary advice for all of these ailments – the quicker they are dealt with, the better.

Companionship

Some people consider getting a puppy when their established dog gets old. This can be a good or bad decision depending on the temperament and nature of the aged dog; if he likes the puppy, then he may gain a new lease of life. If, however, he doesn't, or cannot cope with the puppy's liveliness, he may resent the newcomer and become depressed and withdrawn, stop eating and become ill. If the old dog is the only one in the household and has always been a loner, it would be kinder not to get another dog or puppy as a companion.

Time to say goodbye

Eventually the older dog sleeps more and more and is increasingly reluctant to exercise. While he is able to function normally, if only in this modified way, he is probably quite happy and contented. If his bladder, bowels and limbs begin to fail and he is unable to function without mental distress or physical pain, you must seek veterinary advice, for the only humane thing to do if this is untreatable is to bring this life to an end, allowing him to die painlessly and with dignity. (See pages 124–125 for information on bereavement and euthanasia.)

If your elderly dog displays an increased need for your company, give him plenty of attention and reassurance.

Bereavement

If a much-loved pet dies, or his death is imminent, it often has a deep impact on those humans who loved and cared for him. For many owners, losing a cherished companion is similar to coping with the death of a family member or close friend.

Why pet dogs die

A dog may die for one of two reasons:
• sudden death through accident or illness.
• euthanasia (being 'put to sleep' or 'put down') following an accident or because of incurable illness.

Euthanasia

Other than sudden death, bringing your dog's life to a peaceful end is the most humane way for him to die. A prolonged natural death can be traumatic for both pet and owner, as well as painful for the former. Talk it over with your vet first and decide whether having it done at home or at the vet clinic would be most suitable and practical. Also discuss the options of what to do with your pet's body. Once this has been agreed, then arrange a date – preferably sooner rather than later so as not to prolong your dog's suffering as well as your own.

At the veterinary clinic

Arrange a time when the vet clinic is likely to be quiet, or you can enter and leave through a private entrance so that you do not have to face a waiting room. Have a supportive person drive you there and back; you are likely to be upset, and therefore in no state to drive. Take a blanket in which to wrap your pet to bring him home again if this is what you want to do.

Make the journey there as smooth, stress-free and quiet as possible. If you will be able to bear up in your dog's last moments, then be with him. If you are likely to go to pieces, ask your vet and the vet nurse to deal with it; if you are distressed, it may make your pet equally so and his passing may not be as peaceful as it should be.

At home

This is more expensive, but may be best if you are unable to get to the clinic, your dog is too ill to move, he finds travel upsetting, or you would prefer euthanasia to be done in familiar and comfortable surroundings. On the day, keep your dog's routine beforehand as normal, but give him lots of extra attention and cuddles – he may not understand why you are being extra-affectionate, but may appreciate it, and it will make you feel better.

The process

Properly carried out, the process is quick and relatively painless. A sedative injection may be given if the dog is very distressed or is difficult to handle or restrain. A foreleg is usually shaved to identify where the vein is situated. An overdose of anaesthetic is injected into this vein; the dog becomes drowsy, lapses into unconsciousness and dies peacefully in seconds.

Afterwards

Either the vet will dispose of the body, arrange to have it buried or cremated on your instructions, or you can take it home, if circumstances allow, to bury in the garden. Graves should be at least 1m (3ft 3in) deep and well away from water courses (your local environment agency will be able to advise you). Pet cemeteries and crematoriums will advise you on cost and what is involved.

Grief

Grieving is an essential part of the healing process after bereavement. There is no set limit as to how long owners should grieve: some are able to accept and recover from the loss more easily than others.

Help when you need it most

Sometimes you may feel as though you are over the loss, but then grief hits you again at unexpected moments – such as when something triggers memories of your dog – and feelings of extreme sadness engulf you all over again. Don't be afraid to lean on supportive family and friends when you feel the need, and do make use of the many excellent pet-bereavement support services that are available. If overwhelming sorrow persists longer than you feel able to cope with, go and see an understanding doctor; you may need additional advice, or prescribed medication, to help ease the grief and allow you to function with some normality again.

Children and pet loss

Depending on their age, children react differently to the death of a pet. It will help enormously for a parent to talk things through with a bereavement support befriender as to how to approach and explain pet death. The child too may find

such supportive third-party help invaluable. Avoid saying that the pet was 'put to sleep' as this can create false hope.

Whether a child should be allowed to see the body of the pet depends on the age and the child. A qualified support befriender will be able to advise on the best course of action.

Pet grief

Other animals in the household may also grieve. The best thing to do is to carry on with their routine, and to let them work out a new hierarchy among themselves.

When you feel the time is right to get another dog, remember that there are plenty of homeless dogs waiting in rescue centres for good homes.

Index

Acknowledgements

Managing Editor Clare Churly
Editor Camilla Davis
Executive Art Editor Leigh Jones
Designer Jo Tapper
Picture Library Assistant
  Taura Riley
Assistant Production Controller
  Nosheen Shan

Picture credits
Octopus Publishing Group Ltd 45; /Jane Burton 2, 107, 114-115, 116, 118;
/Stephen Conroy 25; /Steve Gorton 34, 36, 37, 38, 39, 40 top right, 40 bottom, 41
top left, 41 top right, 41 bottom right, 41 bottom left, 42 top centre; /Steve Gorton
42 centre, 43 centre, 43 bottom, 44, 49, 54, 55, 56, 57, 58, 68, 88, 92, 93, 105, 122;
/Rosie Hyde 4, 42 top right, 43 top left, 46, 62, 63, 66 left, 66 centre, 106, 120; /Ray
Moller 8, 12, 13 top, 14, 30; /John Moss 103; /Angus Murray 7, 9, 10, 13 centre, 13
bottom, 20 top right, 20 bottom left, 21, 22, 24, 29, 31, 32 top right, 33, 40 centre
left, 42 top left, 47, 48 top, 50, 51, 59, 59 centre, 59 left 60, 61 bottom, 70, 71, 72,
73, 75 left, 76, 77, 78, 80 left, 80 right, 80 centre, 81 left, 81 right, 82 left, 82 centre,
83 top left, 83 top right, 83 bottom right, 83 bottom left, 84 left, 84 right, 84 right,
84 centre, 85 top left, 85 top right, 85 bottom right, 85 bottom left, 86 top left,
86 top right, 86 bottom, 87 top, 87 bottom right, 87 bottom left, 87 bottom centre,
89 left, 89 right, 90 top right, 90 bottom right, 90 bottom left, 91 top right, 91
bottom right, 91 bottom left; /Tim Ridley 11, 18, 32 top left, 35, 123, 125; /
L Wickenden 23, 26.

Dog
Basics

2